HORRORS OF HELL

Splendors of
HEAVEN

Dr. Michael H. Yeager

5 Fold Media
Visit us at www.5foldmedia.com

Endorsements:

I feel honored to endorse a book that is being used to minister to the church and to lost souls. This new book of Mike Yeager's will change your life. If you have ever had questions about heaven or hell and what they may be like, this book has answers for you. It is not only a true story but lines up with the Word of God on heaven and hell in scriptures such as "the worm shall not die" (see Isa. 66:24) and others.

Not only does Mike passionately give his readers the intimate details of his journey but also gives insightful Scriptures for anyone to receive Jesus as their Savior. I know this book will inspire you to arise from complacency to reach out to a lost world. His book is a catalyst for conquering defeat.

Joanna Coe Herndon
Christian Grace Fellowship

Mike Yeager's testimony unveils the realities of hell and the glories of heaven. This book will stir in you a passion for souls as Mike clearly explains the eternal destiny of those who are lost and without Christ. Sinners are virtually unaware of their march toward the fires of hell. This book is destined to awaken a generation to the realities of heaven, hell and the afterlife.

Gary Bailey

We have known Michael Yeager for over thirty-five years and find him to be a man of integrity, honor, and trust. He is full of God's love and God's Word which have helped him weather storms that have made him a general in the army of God. He has God's heart for souls and God's love for the kingdom and the King. We are blessed to know him, and we recommend him and his work to all who are interested in growing in building God's kingdom on earth as it is in heaven. His apostolic call is evident to us in his unlimited vision and the establishment of ongoing works in this land and others.

Al and Billie Deck
Cedars of Lebanon, Inc.

Dedication:

I dedicate this book to all those who are hungry and thirsty after righteousness; who yearn and long for a harvest of souls, who are waiting for the early and latter rain, and the great and final outpouring of the Holy Ghost. I dedicate this book to all of those who will embrace the fear of the Lord (which is the beginning of wisdom), and at the same time revel In God's love. To those who cry out to be partakers of the heart of the Father, the Son, and the Holy Ghost, whose very heart yearns for the salvation of the multitudes. Oh precious Lord, pour out your Spirit once again upon humanity as in the days of old. May your glorious bride rise up with sickles in their hands, and divine love in their hearts for the lost. The harvest is great, but the laborers are few.

Acknowledgments:

To Jesus Christ my Lord, Savior, and King. Without His divine intervention, I would not be telling about hell; I would be there.

To my one and only precious wife of 33 years, Kathleen Maye Yeager, who has faithfully labored with me in the harvest field all these years, even in the midst of much pain and sorrow.

To my precious five children, Michael, Daniel, Steven, Stephanie and Naomi (who is now with the Lord). They all have worked at my side doing the will of God. May the Lord give them a rich reward. No father could ask for better children.

To all my faithful brothers and sisters at Jesus Is Lord Ministries International.

And a special thanks to my publishers, Andy and Cathy Sanders, who have helped to bring this work to fruition.

CONTENTS

Chapter		Page
1	A Divine Appointment	1
2	My Life Story	13
3	The Journey Begins	25
4	Headed to Hell	35
5	Into the Lava	45
6	Eternity	61
7	No Love	73
8	Out of Hell	87
9	God's Heart Broken	97
10	I Have to Do Something	109
11	In the Harvest	123
12	My Journey to Heaven	129
13	Garden of Eden	137
14	Upon a New Road	147
15	Before the Throne	153
16	The Dream	159
17	Conclusion	163

Chapter 1
A Divine Appointment

Dear reader, before I can take you on this journey I need to clarify a number of issues and facts that might help you understand what happened to me and why it happened. I do not believe that you have picked this book up by mistake or accident. But rather, this is a divine appointment, the providence of God, which has brought us together. What I am about to share with you are two supernatural encounters which the Lord has allowed me to experience. The first was a journey I had to hell. The second part of this book is about when an angel took me to heaven. I believe both of these encounters were explicitly given for the reaping of the harvest. Please understand that God's greatest desire is that souls might be converted. All He has done has been for the salvation of sinners. He came to seek and save the lost.

> *"For the Son of man is come to save that which was lost"* *(Matt. 18:11).*

> *"I will seek that which was lost, and bring again that which was driven away, and will bind up that which was broken, and will strengthen that which was sick"* *(Ezek. 34:16).*

My journey to hell took place in the spring of 1975. You might have the false assumption that an experience

1

that transpired over thirty-five years ago might not have an impact upon my life still. But actually it's the opposite. To this very day, even as I recount this occurrence, it shakes and grips me to the very core of my being. As I reflect upon what the Lord allowed me to experience it is as if I am falling back into hell all over again. I do not know how to fully express how terrifying, frightening, and extremely painful it is. Though it lasted only hours in the physical world, in the spirit realm it seemed as if I was there for an eternity.

> *"For a thousand years in thy sight are but as yesterday when it is past, and as a watch in the night" (Ps. 90:4).*

> *"But, beloved, be not ignorant of this one thing, that one day is with the Lord as a thousand years, and a thousand years as one day"*
> *(2 Pet. 3:8).*

It truly breaks my heart to think of those that I had the misfortune of hearing and seeing, bumping into, and brushing up against as I was in the lake of burning lava. I shudder to think they are still there to this day. And they will be there forever and ever, tormented in the flames of hell. As I have reflected on and pondered my experience, it has caused me to weep many times and wail for hours beyond count through the years. How anyone can say that they have had a revelation of hell or a visitation to hell and not be overwhelmed emotionally, physically, and spiritually, is beyond my comprehension. I cannot speak for others, but for me it is mind-boggling and heart wrenching.

In the last thirty-five years I have been invited and even encouraged to come and speak on this particular experience which the Lord allowed me to have. However, in all of these years I have only gone once to speak at a meeting on this.

Even as I began to share these truths in that meeting I was unable to make it very far before I had to stop.

It has been too painful for me to speak very long in public about my journey to hell. You might think that what I'm about to share with you is extremely exaggerated, but I can tell you without a shadow of a doubt that I am not embellishing in the least. If anything, I find myself at a loss to fully express what hell is really like. I cannot speak for others, but for me it was more real than the flesh and blood world I live in. The Apostle Paul shares with us that he himself experienced this to some extent.

> *"I knew a man in Christ above fourteen years ago (whether in the body, I cannot tell; or whether out of the body, I cannot tell: God knoweth;) such an one caught up to the third heaven. And I knew such a man, (whether in the body, or out of the body, I cannot tell: God knoweth;)" (2 Cor. 12:2-3).*

To me, my experience was both physical and literal. It was not a vision or a dream. I could touch, taste, see, smell, and hear all that transpired. My five senses and my emotional, mental, and psychological perceptions were even more alive in the encounter than they are now. It was as if they were supernaturally enhanced and amplified by God in order for me to experience all of the terrible realities, torments, pains, and agonies of eternal judgment and separation from God.

A Warning

As I take you with me on this journey to hell, do not be surprised if you begin to experience to some degree those things that the Lord has allowed me to encounter.

In the past as I have shared in meetings just small portions of what you are about to read, there have been those who which have begun to sense the smells, sounds, torments, and pains of this terrible and terrifying place; physically, mentally, and emotionally.

In one of these situations there was a minister's wife whom I had known for a significant length of time. For some unknown reason she had approached me on numerous occasions in the past trying to convince me that it was not necessary for God to give such an encounter to His people. I did not argue with her or try to persuade her either way. I have never tried to create or bring about a situation where someone would experience the agonies and torments of hell as I did. I would not wish this on anyone.

This minister and his wife were in a tent revival meeting I was conducting. In this particular meeting the Lord inspired me to speak a little along this line about the pains, sufferings and agonies of eternal damnation. And as I was speaking, this sister in the Lord literally fell out of her chair to the sawdust-covered ground. She began to squirm, twist, scream, and wail. It was the most dreadful and terrible weeping, moaning, and crying you could ever imagine. She continued in this fashion it seemed for over a half an hour. When she was finally able to get her breath and talk, she shared with us in tears and horror what she had experienced. It was not the physical torments of hell. But she had felt the absolute utter hopelessness and total lack of love that is in hell. She now would tell you that she understands what I had experienced and still have been since 1975.

In another meeting in Wisconsin Dells, Wisconsin, I was speaking to an Indian tribe called the Ho-Chunk Nation when strange things began to happen. As I was sharing some of my encounter, a young Indian girl turned to her mother and told her that she was smelling the worst smell

4

she had ever smelled. She said it was like rotten eggs and sulfur. This is not really something that's new. It is reported that when Jonathan Edwards preached his famous sermon "Sinners in the Hands of an Angry God" that those in the meeting could literally feel the flames of hell licking at their feet. Some reported it almost felt as if they were falling through rotten canvas. They could hear the screams and the cries of those in hell. They held on to the front church pews so intensely that their fingers literally turned chalk white. Out of that meeting came a tremendous revival. The Apostle Paul was constantly warning the church about its eternal destiny. He told the body to work out its salvation with fear and trembling.

> *"Therefore watch, and remember, that by the space of three years I ceased not to warn every one night and day with tears" (Acts 20:31).*

> *"Wherefore, my beloved, as ye have always obeyed, not as in my presence only, but now much more in my absence, work out your own salvation with fear and trembling" (Phil. 2:12).*

Divine Encounter

The church of the twenty-first century has lost the understanding that we absolutely need supernatural encounters with the presence of the Lord. From Genesis to Revelation we see encounter after encounter of men and women with the divine supernatural. It is by supernatural visitations and visions that God reveals Himself and His will for humanity. It is also by these divine visitations that He transforms, molds, and shapes His people for a specific task, even as the potter does the clay. The revelation that we have of the Word of God was by divine encounter.

"For the prophecy came not in old time by the will of man: but holy men of God spake as they were moved by the Holy Ghost" (2 Pet. 1:21).

"The Spirit of the LORD spake by me, and his word was in my tongue" (2 Sam. 23:2).

If we were to eliminate every supernatural encounter in the Bible, I dare say there would not be a Bible. If you look at the men and women of God throughout history, those used in any significant way had experienced visions, visitations, translations, and angelic encounters. We could begin with Enoch, Abraham, Jacob, Joseph, Moses, Joshua and Caleb, the judges and continue all the way down through history to the end of the New Testament.

I believe that God wants every one of His people to have a supernatural biblical experience. As you read my journal—this book—you'll discover that if I had not had a divine encounter thirty-five years ago, I may have never been saved and rescued from the powers of darkness. I would have been lost and suffering with those who are in the flames of hell forever. Am I telling you to seek a divine encounter? No; I am saying that as you draw near to God that the veil between the flesh and the Spirit will at times disappear. You will find yourself stepping into the mind-boggling realm of the Spirit. Read Revelation chapter 1 when John was in the Spirit on the Lord's day:

"And I turned to see the voice that spake with me. And being turned, I saw seven golden candlesticks; And in the midst of the seven candlesticks one like unto the Son of man, clothed with a garment down to the foot, and girt about the paps with a golden girdle. His head and his hairs were white like wool, as

white as snow; and his eyes were as a flame of fire; And his feet like unto fine brass, as if they burned in a furnace; and his voice as the sound of many waters. And he had in his right hand seven stars: and out of his mouth went a sharp two-edged sword: and his countenance was as the sun shineth in his strength. And when I saw him, I fell at his feet as dead. And he laid his right hand upon me, saying unto me, Fear not; I am the first and the last: I am he that liveth, and was dead; and, behold, I am alive for evermore, Amen; and have the keys of hell and of death" (Rev. 1:12-18).

The experience I had of going to hell and heaven is not as unusual as some would think it might be. If you read the journals of former revivalists you will discover that in the Welsh revival, John Wesley's revivals, George Whitfield's, Charles Finney's, and many others, masses of people fell to the ground and went into a trance (like a coma) and experienced visions of heaven and hell. It is the Spirit of the Lord that comes upon His people and sinners to reveal divine truths and revelations.

"It is the spirit that quickeneth; the flesh profiteth nothing" (John 6:63).

"Then he answered and spake unto me, saying, This is the word of the LORD unto Zerubbabel, saying, Not by might, nor by power, but by my Spirit, saith the LORD of hosts" (Zech. 4:6).

Let me also add that Scripture says we have not because we ask not. I believe by the Spirit of God, that we need to begin to ask and believe God to give us certain experiences. (We are not seeking these experiences.) These are not experiences that we will consume upon our lust. But these are desires that God would put in our hearts in order to fulfill His divine will in the earth. Whatever we ask of God we must make sure that we believe in our hearts that it is His will and that it is scripturally and biblically correct.

> *"Or what man is there of you, whom if his son ask bread, will he give him a stone? Or if he ask a fish, will he give him a serpent? If ye then, being evil, know how to give good gifts unto your children, how much more shall your Father which is in heaven give good things to them that ask him?" (Matt. 7:9-11).*

I cannot emphasize enough the importance of moving in the power of the Holy Spirit! God never intended us to reap the harvest without the power of His Spirit.

> *"For as the body without the spirit is dead, so faith without works is dead also" (James 2:26).*

> *"And, being assembled together with them, commanded them that they should not depart from Jerusalem, but wait for the promise of the Father, which, saith he, ye have heard of me" (Acts 1:4).*

If we really want to see God move in our lives, families, and churches we need to completely die to all symbolism, traditions, and trappings that would hinder or grieve the Holy Ghost.

> *"O foolish Galatians, who hath bewitched you, that ye should not obey the truth, before*

whose eyes Jesus Christ hath been evidently set forth, crucified among you? This only would I learn of you, Received ye the Spirit by the works of the law, or by the hearing of faith? Are ye so foolish? having begun in the Spirit, are ye now made perfect by the flesh? Have ye suffered so many things in vain? if it be yet in vain. He therefore that ministereth to you the Spirit, and worketh miracles among you, doeth he it by the works of the law, or by the hearing of faith?" (Gal. 3:1-5).

Questions About Hell?

In this book, I hope by God's grace not only to share with you what I experienced in hell, but also hopefully to answer the questions that many may have about why God would create such a place? Why would the godhead (who is love) want people to suffer like this? Why would God send people to such a horrible and terrifying place? Is hell forever? Since God is love why would He make people suffer forever? Does any human being deserve to suffer to this extent? Are devils, demons, and fallen angels in hell? Are the lost souls in hell tormented by devils and demons? Since man is a triune creation, what part of man goes to hell?

"And the very God of peace sanctify you wholly; and I pray God your whole spirit and soul and body be preserved blameless unto the coming of our Lord Jesus Christ" (1 Thess. 5:23).

"For the word of God is quick, and powerful, and sharper than any two-edged sword, piercing even to the dividing asunder of soul

and spirit, and of the joints and marrow, and is a discerner of the thoughts and intents of the heart" (Heb. 4:12).

All of these questions are answered within the Word of God. There are also many other questions, which I have not mentioned, that I believe you will find the answers to by the time you finish reading my story. Some of the things I will be sharing with you will not seem to agree with other numerous books that have been written on this particular subject. I cannot give an answer for these other books or authors. But, as I have determined, I can tell you that not one thing I experienced is contrary to the teachings of scripture, and actually the Bible verifies everything I am about to share with you.

My journey to hell and to heaven took place even before I knew what the Bible had to say on either subject. If either one of these or any of the other experiences I have had through the years had been contrary to the teachings of Christ or the prophets, I would adamantly reject them, turn my back on them, and declare that they were not of God. A God-given vision of heaven or hell or any other visitation would never contradict Scriptures. I am not sharing with you something I made up out of the figment of my own imagination for the purpose of selling books or to make a name for myself. What you are about to read truly happened to me. Please understand that when God gives visions, dreams, and divine encounters that many of these experiences could be revealed by shadows and illustrations of spiritual truths that He wants us to grasp and understand.

"But the fearful, and unbelieving, and the abominable, and murderers, and whoremongers, and sorcerers, and idolaters,

and all liars, shall have their part in the lake which burneth with fire and brimstone: which is the second death" (Rev. 21:8).

Something Is About to Happen

In regards to my journey to heaven, it was similar to my journey to hell in that it did not seem to me to be a vision or a dream. But it was a physical event that was amplified, I'll even say multiplied, beyond that of the normal five senses. I will not be able to share with you all that transpired on this particular journey because the Spirit of God spoke to me things that are not lawful to speak on this side of heaven. But just to give you a "heads up," what God showed me was to take place upon the earth in my lifetime has not yet happened. But I have been sensing with great anticipation in my heart that those hidden events are about to explode upon the pages of human history.

We are about to see things that no other previous generation has seen. For the body of Christ, the church, these events will be amazing, marvelous, wonderful, and yet terrifying. But to those of the world who do not know Christ, it will be like a never-ending horror story and nightmare. We have truly come to the end of the ages.

Not too long ago a young child came to me and told me that he had what he thought was a vision. He described to me an hourglass. He did not know what an hourglass was. But in the very top of the hourglass there was only a very small amount of sand left. I truly believe with all my heart that time is running out. And that what we do for God, and the kingdom, we needed to do quickly.

Where I am about to take you will not tickle or please your flesh. It will not make you want to shout, sing all, or dance. But I believe it'll make you weep and wail for the lost, the damned, and the dying. Why? In order that revival might break forth across the nations. For the Lord of the harvest is patient until He receives the early in latter rain.

"Say not ye, There are yet four months, and then cometh harvest? behold, I say unto you, Lift up your eyes, and look on the fields; for they are white already to harvest" (John 4:35).

Chapter 2
My Life Story

In order to help you to comprehend what you are about to read, I need to give you a quick synopsis of my life. I believe that for all of us God has a divine destiny and purpose, a heavenly plan. I believe that from the moment we are conceived in our mother's womb, the Holy Spirit begins to work in us to bring about the Heavenly Father's perfect will. At the same time, the enemy of our souls and the demonic world is doing all it can to keep us from the revelation of God's purpose for our lives. And if at all possible, it is trying to drag us to hell.

> *"The thief cometh not, but for to steal, and to kill, and to destroy: I am come that they might have life, and that they might have it more abundantly" (John 10:10).*

As human beings we are literally suspended between heaven and hell in a spiritual sense. Every choice we make brings us either closer to hell or to heaven. Our final destiny is really in our own hands. Many have erroneously misunderstood the doctrine of predestination.

> *"Who will have all men to be saved, and to come unto the knowledge of the truth"*
> *(1 Tim. 2:4).*

"The Lord is not slack concerning his promise, as
some men count slackness; but is longsuffering
to us-ward, not willing that any should perish,
but that all should come to repentance"
(2 Pet. 3:9).

The Scriptures cannot be understood with the carnal mind or natural reasoning. What is amazing is that even in our wayward, sinful, and rebellious condition, God moves upon our hearts and lives.

You see, my mother gave birth to me three months early. I was a premature baby with physical disabilities. My lungs were underdeveloped which caused me difficulty in breathing. I remember as a little boy many times looking out through an oxygen tent in a local hospital. My feet also were turned inward, so doctors had to place my feet in braces for approximately five months. My older brother and sister had similar problems with their feet.

The inner bones of my ears were not developed correctly. They were "frozen" in place, and when I became congested, they would not allow the fluids to drain into my sinuses. This created tremendous build up of pressure, which punctured my eardrums, causing a hearing disability.

My tongue was attached to the bottom part of my mouth. I went through numerous operations in order to give me use of it in speech. I was never able to speak fluently even though I went to speech therapy classes. To this day all I can remember of my speech teacher is that she had very large lips. To a great extent most people could not understand a lot of what I was saying. What was most embarrassing is that I could not even say my last name correctly (Yeager). Instead of saying "car," I could only say "cow." Instead of "rat," I would say "wat." Instead of saying "tree," I would say "twee." My tongue simply would not cooperate and flex the way it was meant to. I thank

14

God that after I gave my heart to Jesus Christ and was filled with the Holy Ghost, speaking in tongues, all of these infirmities were healed, including my speech impediment.

Because of these disabilities and to a great extent my very dysfunctional family, I began to get in trouble at an early age. I remember the first time I became intoxicated with alcohol. I was at a cousin's wedding. I was only about seven years old when I became extremely drunk and sick. By the time I was eighteen, I was an alcoholic. This seemed to be a generational curse. Thank God this has been broken over our whole family.

At fifteen years of age I quit school and began to run with a gang. Those in this gang where all older than myself. Our stomping grounds were located right outside of Chicago, between Chicago and Waterford, Wisconsin. We were involved in drugs, stealing, violence, alcohol, and other forms of immorality and wickedness that I will not mention. This led to a life of fear and hate, rebellion, and lawlessness. I had an overwhelming anger expressly for myself. The law finally caught up to me at the age of sixteen, and I was given a choice to either join the military or face prosecution.

I passed my GED (General Education Degree), and I chose to join the Navy. When I first applied, I was turned down because of my hearing disabilities. But our family doctor convinced them that no further harm could happen to my hearing. But because of the immovable bones in my ears, the first time I flew in a high altitude jet my left eardrum burst. I had to be taken to a hospital to have that eardrum replaced.

After I completed boot camp at the Great Lakes Naval base in Illinois, I continued my education in the same location to be an electrician's mate. I graduated at the bottom of my class. My grades were so low that I did not even receive my stripes for E4, which was standard.

Then I was shipped to San Diego, California, for training in the use and the repair of sixteen millimeter projectors. From there I was sent to Adak, Alaska, an island in the Aleutian Island Chain thirteen hundred miles southwest of Anchorage. In the Navy it is considered what is called "sea duty" because of its desolate and remote location. While on Adak my downward spiral continued with an ever-increasing alcohol and drug problem. I began to sell drugs (basically, blonde hashish) in order to support my habit. Then on my nineteenth birthday, February 18, 1975, I had finally come to the end of my road. I was sick of my existence. I hated myself with all of my shortcomings and all of my failures. In my opinion my whole life was nothing but one, big fat zero. All I could see was the foolishness of my life, the vanity of my existence. I did not want to live another day, not another hour, or even another minute. At this time in my life I did not realize that there were demonic powers which were out to destroy me and drag my soul to hell.

Suicide

The only way of escape that I could see was for me to kill myself. My older brother (by four years) had tried to commit suicide when he was about eighteen years old by taking an overdose of medicine. I remember finding him on the floor of our living room looking as if he was already dead. I called for an ambulance, and thank God, they arrived in time to pump his stomach. It was not even a year later when I found my older sister (by two years) in the same condition. Thank God, once again they arrived in time to save my sister. I had determined in my heart that I was not going to make the same mistake that my brother and sister had made.

Prior to this I had gone to a local hardware and hunting store and purchased a very sharp, large survival knife. The thought entered my mind that with this knife I could escape my useless and horrible life. I waited until there was no one left in our barracks. I went into what we call "the head" in the Navy, which is another word for the bathroom. I put that knife to my wrist with every intent and purpose of slitting my wrist, cutting down through my arteries, and ending my miserable life.

I remember weeping uncontrollably, feeling sorry for myself. But as I began to apply pressure to the knife against my wrist, *all of a sudden* something mysterious and supernatural happened. It was as if an invisible blanket came floating down through the ceiling of that little bathroom, floating down on top of me. I could feel it. To me it was very real, physical, and tangible. In one single moment an overwhelming, heart-stopping, mind-boggling fear hit me like a ton of bricks. It was what I now know as the fear of the Lord. I had never known the fear of the Lord before this experience. But at that very moment by the Spirit of God I knew that I knew, that I was going to hell. I knew that I deserved hell; I knew that I belonged in hell. I knew that I had sinned against a holy and righteous God. Hell was reaching out for me. I knew that hell had a right to claim me. At that moment I did not know why I knew this, but I knew it. I remember beginning to shake so violently under this conviction—this reality—that I dropped my knife into the sink.

> *"The fear of the LORD is the beginning of wisdom" (Prov. 9:10).*

> *"My flesh trembleth for fear of thee; and I am afraid of thy judgments" (Ps. 119:120).*

The Scriptures declare that at the end of the age the fear of the Lord would depart from the earth. A number of years ago as I was preparing for a Sunday morning service (I have been a pastor now for over thirty years), the Spirit of the Lord spoke to me. He asked me what I thought was a very simple question. He said to me, "Son, why did Lucifer fall?" I thought for a moment and replied, "Lord, because he wanted to be God." This answer is biblically correct, but I discovered that there is more to it than just that.

> *"How art thou fallen from heaven, O Lucifer, son of the morning! how art thou cut down to the ground, which didst weaken the nations! For thou hast said in thine heart, I will ascend into heaven, I will exalt my throne above the stars of God: I will sit also upon the mount of the congregation, in the sides of the north: I will ascend above the heights of the clouds; I will be like the most High. Yet thou shalt be brought down to hell, to the sides of the pit"*
> *(Is. 14:12-15).*

Once again the Spirit of God asked me the same question, "Why did Lucifer fall?" Again I answered the same. The Lord asked me a third time, "Son, why did Lucifer fall?" I finally answered with, "Lord, I don't know. Would You please tell me why he fell?" The Lord spoke to me and said, "Because none of the angelic realm, the spiritual realm, or creation itself had ever seen My wrath, My anger, or vengeance. All they had ever known was My goodness and love." Satan and his followers did not maintain the fear of the Lord in their hearts. The Lord told me that this present generation is making the exact same terrible mistake! He said, "They do not understand that I am a consuming fire." This is one reason that the church is rampant with sin and disobedience to God and His holy Word. God is a holy and righteous God. He cannot allow sin to continue.

"For our God is a consuming fire" (Heb. 12:29).

"Follow peace with all men, and holiness, without which no man shall see the Lord"
(Heb. 12:14).

Throughout eternity not only will the saints walk in the love of Christ, but they will forever have built within them the fear of the Lord. The fear of the Lord is not a curse. It is a divine gift from the heavenly Father. It is placed within the heart of the saint in order to keep him within the will of God to protect him from the lies and deceptions of that which is evil.

"And they shall be my people, and I will be their God: And I will give them one heart, and one way, that they may fear me for ever, for the good of them, and of their children after them: And I will make an everlasting covenant with them, that I will not turn away from them, to do them good; but I will put my fear in their hearts, that they shall not depart from me. Yea, I will rejoice over them to do them good, and I will plant them in this land assuredly with my whole heart and with my whole soul"
(Jer. 32:38-41).

Childhood Experience

There was only one other time I could remember having experienced a supernatural visitation. I was about six years old. Even during those years, I had caused my parents all kinds of heartache and sorrow. I was always getting into trouble, yelling, screaming, cursing, and disobeying. I caused my mother, Shirley, so much heartache that once, in utter frustration, she told me that I had to be the devil himself. She never knew how those words deeply affected me. No matter how hard I tried to be good, I just got worse. I remember as a little boy I would get up on the sink in our little bathroom, look in the mirror, and run my hands through my hair. I was absolutely positive that I could feel two large lumps beginning to form on my skull. I was almost positive that I was the devil himself.

One night during this time I had gotten up to go to the bathroom. It was a cold winter night, and there was at least a foot of snow on the ground. The house was very quiet because everyone else in my family was sleeping. The light of the moon was shining through the bathroom window. The window was made of milk-colored, perforated glass. As I looked through it, a shiver ran from my head to my feet. There in the milk-colored glass I saw three crosses. The middle one seemed to be three-dimensional. An overwhelming sense of love radiated from the middle cross. Then as I looked at it very intently, I thought there was a figure of a man hanging on it. I saw blood flowing from his hands and feet and his head. The next thing I knew, I was crying. I wept uncontrollably and did not understand what it was all about. Yet somehow I knew that God had touched me.

For the next two weeks, I was totally different, almost a saint. I believe it was because of this experience that I began to have the desire to be a Roman Catholic priest. My mother was completely amazed at the change that overtook me. I became very polite, kind, and helpful. No one had to ask me to help; I simply did it. And even when the other children mocked me, I just ignored them instead of fighting back. I even quit aggravating my sister, Debbie. But I'm sorry to say that this did not last very long. Before I knew it I became worse than I was before.

This spiritual experience as a child, this encounter that I had with God, was forgotten as if it had never happened.

Now here I was, thirteen years later, experiencing another supernatural visitation while trying to kill myself. But this was much stronger. I turned my back on that sink, walked out of that little bathroom, and threw myself down on the floor next to my military bunk. The presence of God was so real I could barely breathe or move.

New Creation

As I cried out to Jesus, He supernaturally stepped into my life. It was as if a bolt of lightning hit me. Love, supernatural awesome love, began to roll over me, wave after wave after glorious wave. Instantly in my heart I knew without a shadow of a doubt that God loved me, died for me, rose from the dead, and was coming back for me. It was as if buckets of tangible love poured over the top of me and into me. I went from mind-boggling, overwhelming fear to an absolute, complete, and overwhelming love. Jesus set me free completely and instantly. I was free from the desire and need to do drugs! I was free from alcohol! I was free from ungodly desires! I was free from chewing tobacco and three packs of cigarettes a day! The overwhelming depression, self-pity, and self-loathing were gone. The emptiness that I had experienced and tried to fill with everything the world had to offer—alcohol and drugs, pornography and sex, fast cars and sports, materialism and money, violence and fighting—was now filled with an eternal quality, the presence of Christ in my heart.

> *"Therefore if any man be in Christ, he is a new creature: old things are passed away; behold, all things are become new"* *(2 Cor. 5:17).*

I was so radically changed and transformed by the Spirit, by the power of God, that I fell in love with

Christ head over heels. There is no way that I could ever do enough to express my love and devotion or the gratefulness that was in my heart for Jesus at that moment. For the first time in my life I knew what love was, or should I say who love is. It is the Father, the Son, and the Holy Ghost. And now because Jesus Christ lives in my heart it has created within me an amazing, overwhelming love for others. I received an overwhelming desire to go out and to tell others about Jesus Christ and what He had done for me.

> *"And hope maketh not ashamed; because the love of God is shed abroad in our hearts by the Holy Ghost which is given unto us" (Rom. 5:5).*

Not only had He rescued me from an immoral life, from suicide, and from hell, but within a short period of time I was healed of all of my physical ailments and disabilities.

> *"Who his own self bare our sins in his own body on the tree, that we, being dead to sins, should live unto righteousness: by whose stripes ye were healed" (1 Pet. 2:24).*

> *"That it might be fulfilled which was spoken by Esaias the prophet, saying, Himself took our infirmities, and bare our sicknesses" (Matt. 8:17).*

Immediately I began to devour the Word of God, especially the four gospels, Matthew, Mark, Luke, and John. Daily I grew in my knowledge of God's awesome goodness and love and the wonderful plan He has for you and me. But within my heart I knew that there had to be a greater level of love and compassion and concern for the lost, the damned, the doomed, and the dying. There had to be a deeper level for those who were blind and ignorant of their spiritual condition even as I had been. So I began to cry out to God intensely, asking Him to allow me to have a supernatural experience of hell. I wanted this in order that I would have a greater and deeper compassion, a deeper love, a deeper understanding for the lost. I truly wanted to know the pains, the sorrows, the torments, the fears, and the agonies of those in hell. I wanted to weep and wail, to travail in a broken heart over the unconverted in order to reach them more effectively. I did not realize at this time that it was the Holy Spirit who was putting this prayer in my mouth. Paul proclaimed:

"My little children, of whom I travail in birth again until Christ be formed in you" (Gal. 4:19).

"Be in pain, and labour to bring forth, O daughter of Zion, like a woman in travail" (Mic. 4:10a).

The Spirit of the Lord began to take me into deep and fervent intercessory prayer. He began to teach me how to stand in the gap on behalf of others, to walk the floor for hours on end for souls. He taught me how to lay upon my face in His presence until there was a breakthrough. He showed me how to submit my body as an instrument, a vessel He could pray through. Every believer, every child of God is called to intercede and travail for souls. It has been said that there is power in prayer. I know what people mean when they make that statement, but it's not exactly accurate. There are many religions in which people pray obsessively. But of course it brings no good results. The power does not come from the prayer, but the power comes from the One that we are crying out to! Jesus declared:

"I am the vine, ye are the branches: He that abideth in me, and I in him, the same bringeth forth much fruit: for without me ye can do nothing" (John 15:5).

23

Chapter 3
The Journey Begins

As I mentioned earlier, there is an island in the Aleutian chain called Adak, Alaska, which is known for its numerous earthquakes. This island is where I was stationed in the military as an electrician's mate third class. The Navy base had a top-secret military installation and was used as a harbor for submarines and ships. The top-secret installation was so hush-hush that most of us on the base did not really know what was taking place there. When I first arrived on the base, I quickly had to get used to the tremors and continual earthquakes. There were times I experienced tremors and quakes so strong they would wake me out of my sleep. My bed would shake so violently that I thought I was going to fall out of it.

I remember one night when I first arrived I was sleeping very soundly. All of a sudden my bed not only began to shake, but it was literally bouncing up and down like a rubber ball. I thought it was the men in my barracks playing a newbie trick on me. I automatically began to yell for them to stop before I opened my eyes. But when I opened my eyes and looked around no one was there. That was how much the building shook.

Now, one night I was deep in prayer with Willy, an African American brother in my barracks. I had the privilege of seeing Willie come back to Christ. At one time previously he had walked with the Lord but had backslid.

25

Before and after he was saved our nickname for him was "Willy Wine" because now he was filled with new wine. Now, as we were praying together, something very strange and very frightening began to happen to me. At the time of this event there was a gathering of some men in our battalion. They were having a party in the common area right outside our sleeping quarters where we were praying. The party they were having was quite loud with music and laughter, but it did not hinder us from crying out to God for souls.

As we were praying, I could sense that something was about to happen. The hair on the back of my arms and neck stood up on end. It was as if electricity was filling the very atmosphere around us. I sensed a strong tugging to go deeper in prayer. I gave myself completely over to the spirit of intercession, crying out to the Lord once again to experience the sorrows and agonies of hell. Please understand that I believe God put this desire, this prayer, into my heart for the love of souls. I began to pray in a realm that I had never been in before when suddenly an overwhelming and tangible darkness descended upon me.

> *"And when the sun was going down, a deep sleep fell upon Abram; and, lo, an horror of great darkness fell upon him" (Gen. 15:12).*

A frightening darkness enveloped me. Everything around me disappeared. I no longer heard the music or the party that was taking place. Even though Willie was right there with me, I did not hear or see him. And it seemed as if time itself had come to a stop. To my utter shock, amazement, and horror, the floor and the building around me began to shake more violently than I had ever experienced before. Usually when we did get a quake it would only last a matter of seconds. But in this situation the shaking did not stop as it normally did, rather it increased.

26

All I could do at this moment was to try to hug the floor and hang on for dear life. The darkness lifted, but I could not see Willie anywhere. Then a terrible ripping and grinding noise filled the air. I saw the floor of the barracks ripple like that of a wave on the sea. The very floor of the barracks that I was laying upon began to tear and rip apart. I watched in stunned amazement and horror as the floor tiles popped and stretched. The concrete and steel within the building began to twist and rip apart. And the floor I was laying on began to split and tear open right below me.

I immediately began to look for a way to get out of the building. Everything was shaking so violently that I could not get up off the floor to make a dash to escape. The dust and dirt in the room was so thick and heavy that I could hardly breathe. Now this rip in the floor began to enlarge and became an opening. I would call it more like a hole. I began to slip and fall into this hole; I tried desperately to reach for any kind of handhold that I could find. I began to scream and yell for help. But there was no one to help me. I became more and more desperate trying to grab hold of something, anything that I could get my hands on. Objects around me began to fall through this hole in the floor. I watched as physical objects slipped past me into this hole. And I could feel myself sliding more and more.

No matter how desperately I was trying to cling to and hold on to items to prevent my falling, there was nothing that I could do. Finally, I slipped and fell backward as if falling off a ladder. As I was falling, everything seemed to go into slow motion like film that is slowed for a preview. I was falling with parts of the crumbling building all around me. I watched as I fell past twisted steel beams, concrete floors, walls ripped into pieces, plumbing and heating pipes, and sparking electric wires. I went past the underground tunnels that connected the buildings together.

27

The next thing that I knew I was falling past the ground and rock of the island. This terrible rip in the earth, this hole that I was falling down began to take on the form and similarity of that of a well, like an endless tube, an ever-proceeding pit. It became approximately three feet wide. As I was falling, I was desperately trying to grab hold of the rocks that were protruding from the sides of this deep dark pit, but my descent was too fast. None of the rocks seemed to protrude far enough for me to get a good handhold.

Even as I was falling down this hole I was not experiencing any fear of going to hell or fear of dying because I had a calm assurance that I knew my heart was right with God. I was ready to meet my Savior. Don't misunderstand; I am not saying that I had no fear! Though I knew in my heart that I was right with God, I was still filled with the absolute horror of not knowing what was happening to me. *At that moment I did not have any idea whatsoever that I was plunging into hell.*

I kept trying to figure out how I could stop my descent into this hole. What I was experiencing was mind-boggling because to me it was truly physically happening. I could feel, touch, smell, hear, and see everything that was happening to me. Actually everything seemed to be amplified beyond my normal five senses. Through the years I had experienced dreams, nightmares, and hallucinations from drugs and alcohol which I had taken, but none of them came anywhere near to what I was experiencing at that very moment. My mind kept screaming, *How can I stop my descent into this hole?* I just kept on falling down and down into this really deep dark hole. Deeper and deeper I fell—down, down, down. I must have fallen mile after mile.

Here are some facts that you might be interested in. From any given point upon the surface of the earth, it is close to four thousand miles to the earth's core center. The terminal velocity of a skydiver with no parachute is about 124 miles per hour, or 200 kilometers per hour.[1] Conceivably, if the center of the earth were hollow, it would take you approximately thirty-two hours to fall to the center.

"He hath said, which heard the words of God, which saw the vision of the Almighty, falling into a trance, but having his eyes open"
(Num. 24:4).

Terrible Stink

Now as I was falling down this deep dark hole, a violent and overwhelming hot wind began blowing from somewhere at the bottom of this shaft and hitting me in the face. It was a suffocating, nauseating, stinking wind. It smelled of rotting eggs and sulfur. It became almost impossible for me to breathe. I tried to use my shirt as a mask to filter out the stinking smell. But it was to no avail.

When I was in the Navy in basic training, part of our training was that we were all forced to go through a facility that had been especially designed like that of the interior of a naval vessel. This building had very small corridors and long hallways. The conditions simulated that of a fire burning on the inside of the ship. The building was pumped full of smoke and heat. What we were to endeavor to do was to make it through this building in complete darkness from one side to the other. It may not sound very frightening or physically grueling, but it was. A number of the men panicked and passed out. A rescue team went in to rescue them before they died from carbon monoxide poisoning. Of course this team went in with breathing equipment. For sure that experience was frightening and even dangerous, but what was taking place to me now was much more horrifying than what I had experienced then.

*"Their slain also shall be cast out, and their
stink shall come up out of their carcases, and
the mountains shall be melted with their blood"
(Isa. 34:3).*

Actually this experience in and of itself should have
been enough to kill me. I kept trying to get a breath of fresh
air, but there was none to be had. As I was desperately trying
to breathe I continued to fall. How long I fell down this hole
I do not know. But it seemed to me to have no end, to be
bottomless. Or was it? As I looked down in the direction that
I was falling feet first, I looked between my feet. I began to
see a very small and very faint orange, yellowish, reddish
glow. It began extremely small, but as I continued to fall
toward the light it became brighter and brighter.

Never-Ending Cavern

Before I knew it I was out of this black hole, this
tunnel. I had entered into a humongous and gigantic,
seemingly never-ending cavern. I could see no end in sight.
It was as if I had fallen into a whole different world, an
underworld. I was falling like a skydiver. Now, I was tens
of thousands of feet above an ocean of liquefied, swirling
lava and blazing fire.

Thousands of feet below me was a frightening, boiling
lake of fire. It was burning, churning, and bubbling, almost
similar to that of a pan of overheated boiling molasses on
a stove. I could see that it was extremely aggravated and
violent. It was almost as if it was filled and possessed
with an aggressive, living fury. Fire and brimstone were
exploding upon its surface in every direction sending
flames rising thousands of feet into the air. The flames
darted here and there like a huge blazing gasoline fire. It
would appear one moment in one area, vanish, and then

appear somewhere else. At the same time there were air-shattering explosions, like volcanoes erupting across this vast surface of liquefied lava. It was like a living, swirling, obsessed whirlpool of fire, brimstone, and lava. It glowed different colors of red, orange, and yellow.

Perhaps a better description would be that it pulsated and radiated like hot charcoal in a furnace, with molten steel, liquefied stone, and swirling gases. Fire danced across the top of its surface like miniature tornadoes spinning violently out of control. They would spin until they ascended up into the black nothingness of the cavern I was falling in.

Intense Heat

As I continued to descend toward the surface of this ocean, this endless lake of liquid fire and lava. It seemed to me that I was about ten thousand feet above the surface of this ocean. And even at ten thousand feet, the heat that was hitting me was so intense that my very flesh felt as if it was withering, melting, and burning. It felt as if it was being ripped off of my hands, my face, and my body. In the past I have received minor burns whether it was from cooking or from building a fire to keep the house warm. But that was minor—a mosquito bite compared to what was happening to me now. As I looked at my skin and flesh it was beginning to bubble and blister. My whole body was beginning to burn. My clothes were catching on fire, and I could not put them out. My shoes were melting to my feet. My hair caught on fire like the wick on a candlestick. It was as if someone had doused me with gasoline and then threw a match on me. I began to scream like a madman.

At the beginning of this book, I asked how could anyone truly have experienced what I am sharing with you and yet not be shaken to the very core of their being

31

every time they retell their story? I'm telling you that as I recount to you what transpired, my heart is filled with dread and trembling. At that same time my lungs felt like they were going to be burned out of my chest. I needed cool fresh air, but there was none to be had. Can you imagine what it would be like to be roasted alive slowly over an open burning pit with red hot coals? This is what I was experiencing.

Since then I have done a little bit of scientific research. I was amazed that my experience was not only biblically in line with the Scriptures but also scientifically accurate. Here are some facts about colors and temperatures I discovered:

> *By way of its color, incandescent rock gives a crude estimate of temperature. For example, orange-to-yellow colors are emitted when rocks (or melt) are hotter than about 900 degrees Celsius (1,650 degrees Fahrenheit). Dark-to-bright cherry red is characteristic as material cools to 630 degrees Celsius (1,165 degrees Fahrenheit). Faint red glow persists down to about 480 degrees Celsius (895 degrees Fahrenheit). For comparison, a pizza oven is operated at temperatures ranging from 260 to 315 degrees Celsius (500 to 600 degrees Fahrenheit). Different metals have different melting points. Here are some examples in degrees: Lead melts at 327.5; aluminum at 660; gold at 5,505; copper at 1,084; nickel at 1453; and iron at 1,535.* [2]

Dreadful Screams

In the midst of this overwhelming pain and agony, my ears began to be filled with a strange, eerie sound—a humming sound, like a throbbing deep, moan that never stopped. As I was falling closer and closer to the surface of the burning lava, this humming, groaning, moaning sound increased in its intensity. It became an ear-piercing, overwhelming, never-ending sound that grew louder and louder. It was as if my head was surrounded by a huge hive of angry bees. As I continued to fall toward this churning, massive ocean, the sound that I was hearing became more distinct and clear. It contained ear-piercing highs and incredible heartbreaking lows with many other pitches in between that are too numerous to describe to you. I remember asking myself in my pain and torment, "What in the world can this sound be that I am hearing? What could be causing such terrible heart wrenching, horror-filled sounds?" And then at that very moment I believe that the Spirit of the Lord opened up my understanding to what was happening to me. It hit me like an eighteen-wheel truck slamming into my body.

The sound that I was hearing was not coming from equipment, machinery or something from nature. But it was coming from human beings, my friend. The sound that was coming to my ears was from human beings who were screaming, wailing, groaning, and moaning with an incredible, intense, overwhelming pain. They were in unbelievable agony with unbearable torments. My ears were filled with the terrible screams of damned souls.

"Therefore I will wail and howl, I will go stripped and naked" (Mic. 1:8).

"And shall cast them into a furnace of fire: there shall be wailing and gnashing of teeth"
(Matt. 13:42).

I remember my whole body began to shake violently almost as if I were having convulsions. It was like rivers of absolute dismay and complete horror. The bitter lamentations of suffering humanity engulfed me. Oh how their sorrows flooded my very being. Even as I retell this story to you it is as if my heart is being ripped out of my chest. And the agony and pain that I am experiencing right now is nothing compared to the agony that God is experiencing. You see, it is His will that none should perish. But all should have eternal life.

> *"O Jerusalem, Jerusalem, which killest the prophets, and stonest them that are sent unto thee; how often would I have gathered thy children together, as a hen doth gather her brood under her wings, and ye would not!"* *(Luke 13:34).*

Chapter 4
Headed to Hell

I had not understood or realized what was really happening to me. The Spirit of God must have been keeping my mind and heart blind to what was happening in order that it might create a greater impact upon my life. But now, at this very moment and second with a mind-numbing shock, I realized that God had heard my prayers. God had, for some strange reason, answered my cry quite literally. There was no turning back. There was no stopping what had begun. At the terminal velocity of 124 miles an hour I was headed straight for the unbelievable torments and sufferings of hell—the terrible lake of fire which was right below me.

There is a growing population of those who say that they do not believe in hell. But the foolish objections of the spiritual blind will not do away with hell. There are many false doctrines and philosophies in the modern-day church. And there are so-called ministers of the Gospel who say there is no hell or that the souls of men will not burn forever but will be burned up. Many are beginning to distort the Scriptures in order to try to prove that there is not such a thing as eternal damnation. There are even those who believe that all will be saved in the end, including the devil and his angels. Some teach that there is a place called purgatory. It is a place that believers go in order to be purged by the fires and torments, believing such a place will cleanse the heart and the soul of a believer. In my

35

experience of going to hell there was no such place called purgatory. Neither is there anywhere within the Scriptures that teach of such a place.

Once you end up in hell, all the money and wealth of the world can never get you out. Please listen to me, these are all lies, propagated by the devil and his demons. The enemy of our souls wants you to believe his lies that your soul might be damned. The Scriptures cannot lie. And within the Scriptures it clearly declares and describes the reality of hell.

> *"And the smoke of their torment ascendeth up for ever and ever: and they have no rest day or night" (Rev. 14:11).*

> *"If anyone's name was not found in the book of life, he was thrown into the lake of fire"*
> *(Rev. 20:15).*

> *"Therefore hell hath enlarged herself, and opened up her mouth without measure: and their glory, and their multitude, and their pomp, and he that rejoiceth, shall descend into it"*
> *(Isa. 5:14).*

Hell is not a respecter of people—of gender, color, race, position, wealth, or education. You see, my friend, Jesus Christ spoke a lot about hell. Jesus spoke on hell ten times more than He did about heaven. Who is Jesus Christ to the believer? He is our everything, our very life and breath, our all in all. He is the foundation upon which we build our very existence. All of our eternal and immortal hopes are placed upon Him.

> *"And are built upon the foundation of the apostles and prophets, Jesus Christ himself being the chief corner stone" (Eph. 2:20).*

"Neither is there salvation in any other: for there is none other name under heaven given among men, whereby we must be saved" (Acts 4:12).

"When Christ, who is our life, shall appear, then shall ye also appear with him in glory" (Col. 3:4).

The words of Christ must take complete and absolute superiority over all else! It really doesn't matter who proclaims or declares that there is no hell. For Jesus Christ, our Lord and Master, the author and finisher of our salvation, declares otherwise. Look at what Jesus declared in the gospels:

"And if thy right eye offend thee, pluck it out, and cast it from thee: for it is profitable for thee that one of thy members should perish, and not that thy whole body should be cast into hell. And if thy right hand offend thee, cut it off, and cast it from thee: for it is profitable for thee that one of thy members should perish, and not that thy whole body should be cast into hell"
(Matt. 5:29-30).

"But the children of the kingdom shall be cast out into outer darkness: there shall be weeping and gnashing of teeth" (Matt. 8:12).

"The Son of man shall send forth his angels, and they shall gather out of his kingdom all things that offend, and them which do iniquity; And shall cast them into a furnace of fire: there shall be wailing and gnashing of teeth" (Matt. 13:41-42).

My friends, please listen to me, hell is real. The Bible says that hell is:

- A great fire
- A fierce fire
- An irresistible fire
- A continual fire
- A dark fire
- An unquenchable fire
- An everlasting fire

Why People Are in Hell

People are in hell because of rebellion and disobedience to God. It is what the Bible calls sin. And what is sin? It is when you live by the standard of this: Not God's will be done, but my will be done. It is living a self-centered life, which is the gateway to hell.

It is the broad and wide path that leads men to eternal damnation, to separation from God where there is never-ending anguish, unutterable sorrows, everlasting pain, and eternal torments.

> *"Enter ye in at the strait gate: for wide is the gate, and broad is the way, that leadeth to destruction, and many there be which go in thereat" (Matt. 7:13).*

Sin is being self-pleasing, self-loving, self-obsessed, self-centered, self-serving, and self-seeking. It is the vain pursuit of ungodly pleasures. Sin is rebellion and mutiny, and disobedience to God and His holy Word. It is that which is contrary to God's divine nature and His character, spitting in the very face of the One who died for us and gave Himself for us. Those in sin make themselves god, sitting upon the throne of their own heart with no pursuit of the Father's will. I beg you with all the sincerity of my heart, that if you do not know Jesus Christ in a personal, intimate way, please turn to Christ right now and come out of your sins. Turn from your self-pleasing and wicked ways. Please change your mind, and give Jesus your heart, soul, life, mind, and body. We need to give all of our selves to Jesus, even as He gave all of Himself for us! Jesus, by His own divine nature, will give you complete and total victory over the satanic nature.

> *"Whereby are given unto us exceeding great and precious promises: that by these ye might be partakers of the divine nature, having escaped the corruption that is in the world through lust" (2 Pet. 1:4).*

You see God became a man and gave Himself as the ultimate sacrifice for our sins. Thereby providing the victory we need to overcome the world, flesh, and the devil.

> *"For this purpose the Son of God was manifested, that he might destroy the works of the devil" (1 John 3:8).*

He died to save our souls and to resurrect and create His divine image and nature into our hearts once again. We must determine in our hearts to give Him all that we are, all that we have, and all that we will ever be. We have borne the image of the earthly fallen Adam. Now we must bear the image of the heavenly Adam. Beloved, are you walking on the broad and wide way of sin, which leads to eternal destruction? Or are you walking on the straight and narrow pathway of loving God, loving holiness, loving faith, and loving obedience?

"The wicked shall be turned into hell, and all the nations that forget God" (Ps. 9:17).

"The way of life is above to the wise, that he may depart from hell beneath" (Prov. 15:24).

You see, my friend, we will all someday die. It does not matter who you are or what you possess. You and I will die.

"For what is your life? It is even a vapour, that appeareth for a little time, and then vanisheth away" (James 4:14).

Now here I am, God has heard my prayer, and I am falling toward the lake of fire, the ocean of damnation, at over 124 miles an hour.

Bobbing Corks

At about two thousand feet above the surface of the ocean of hell, the pain that was hitting my body was overwhelming, unbearable, unbelievable, and all consuming. My lungs were on fire. My eyes felt like they were being burned out of my sockets. My clothes had burned and melted to my flesh. I was beyond third-degree burns.

And yet, incredibly I was still fully aware of everything that was transpiring around me. If anything, my five senses were more alive than ever before. I believe that God must have supernaturally increased my capacity to experience all that I was going through.

I was looking down in the direction in which I was headed. I could see upon the surface of the lake of fire what looked like little black objects violently bobbing up and down like fishing corks in the orange and red glow of the burning, churning, bubbling ocean of hell. As my eyes became more focused (by the grace of God), I could see thousands upon tens of thousands of these objects dotting the surface. They were everywhere. As I looked upon them, I found myself possessed by an overwhelming curiosity. I lost interest in everything else that was happening to me.

Even though I was experiencing tremendous and unbelievable pain and agony, I was still able to focus my mind and attention upon these objects. My mind was very clear and sharp. The only way to describe my curiosity was that it was supernatural. This curiosity gripped my mind and heart. And as I fell closer and closer, I could see that these objects were actually oblong, not round as I had thought. But they contained limbs at both ends. And these limbs were waving back and forth, back and forth, in a frantic jerking type of motion. Out of my innermost being, I let out a deep, tormented groan as I suddenly realized what I was looking at. These black, bobbing objects were nothing less than human beings! People! They were masses of humanity from every nation, culture, tribe, and tongue. And they were screaming, moaning, and yelling as they were being turned and tossed about, head over heels, carried along in the swirling lava of the burning, churning, undercurrents of hell.

Now, in my past I have heard people weeping and wailing, crying over the death of a precious loved one. I have experienced this myself when our four-and-a-half-year-old little girl, Naomi, died. That same year my mother died. I wailed and wept and cried. But never had I heard crying like this, such agony, such screaming, such sorrow. The wailing and howls of pain broke my heart. It still breaks my heart to this day as I think upon this experience. I could not tell by looking upon these burning blackened masses of humanity who or what they were. It was only by the Spirit of God that I discern these truths. For when their physical body hit the flaming fires of hell they lost their sexuality. They lost their nationality, their race and color of skin. No longer could you determine what their age was. For hell makes all people equal.

Dreadful Screams

These are souls forever damned. These are souls with no hope, escape, help, or relief from pain. Maybe these are people you and I have known—dads and moms, brothers and sisters, aunts and uncles, neighbors and friends who have died without loving Christ. Their hearts were full of the cares and lusts of this world. Their lives were full of selfishness and sin. They had no time for God or His Word. They spent their lives pursuing the useless pleasures of this world, filling their minds with vain and useless amusements, foolish entertainment, ungodly movies, involving themselves in immoral activities. The Apostle Paul warned us:

> *"Know this also, that in the last days perilous times shall come" (2 Tim. 3:1).*

There will be a time that will be very dangerous and difficult to be a Christian. People will become totally self-centered, and because people are self-centered they will love money. They will be lifted up with pride. They will be quick to speak bitter words. They will have no respect for parents and be thankless, ungrateful, and wicked. They will not even care about their own families. Many will be hard-hearted, unforgiving, slanderers; they will be critical and find fault in others. People will be without self-control and be ugly and nasty in their attitudes with no love for what is right or good. Some will even betray their own friends. Many will be stubborn and bloated with self-importance. They will love the useless pleasures and amusements of this world more than God.

"For many walk, of whom I have told you often, and now tell you even weeping, that they are the enemies of the cross of Christ: Whose end is destruction, whose God is their belly, and whose glory is in their shame, who mind earthly things" (Phil. 3:18-19).

My friend, either we love God and forsake the world or we love the world and forsake God. We cannot love, follow, and obey both of them. Christ gave all of Himself, and now He wants all of us!

These people who are in hell at this very moment God called for so long, loud, and often with such great fervency. Maybe He is calling you right now in the same way. And yet they closed their ears. They were blind and deaf to the warnings of God. Death chased them even as maybe it does you right now. The wrath of God hung over their heads. Yet they cared not, and they feared not. None of these things seemed to move them. It did not trouble their hearts that they did not love God or obey Him. They ate and drank. They bought and sold. They planted and built, and they went to work and came home. Some even went to church, but went on sinning and living as if they would never die. Some were ignorant and senseless of their danger. They thought that God was nothing but mercy and forgiveness. No matter how sinful they lived their lives, they thought that the blood of Jesus would forgive them of sins that they refused to give up and come out of. They did not realize that God hates sin, and that He is holy, jealous, and righteous.

"Follow peace with all men, and holiness, without which no man shall see the Lord" (Heb. 12:14).

> *"Having therefore these promises, dearly beloved, let us cleanse ourselves from all filthiness of the flesh and spirit, perfecting holiness in the fear of God" (2 Cor. 7:1).*

And because He is a righteous God, He must judge sin. By the time that these people discovered this truth it was too late. For they died and woke up in a dreadful, boiling lake of brimstone, sulfur, and fire. They have no way of escape, no relief from pain, and no hope for the future. These people have nothing to look forward to except endless torment, loneliness, and pain. Their bodies burned black like burnt chicken that had been overcooked on a barbecue pit. The unquenchable flames of a never-ending hell blackened their souls. Those down there looked like living and moving pieces of charcoal.

Chapter 5
Into the Lava

Because I was so caught-up in the stark reality of what was going on before me, I did not realize that I was still falling closer and closer to the surface of the lake of fire. Suddenly, I plunged into the lava. It was like burning mud and quicksand. Immediately it sucked me in with a frightening ferocity. It engulfed me, pulling me down, swallowing me up in its hideous stomach of endless suffering and pain. It covered me over and filled my mouth and my nose, ears and my eyes with an overwhelming, intense burning pain. The flaming sulfur of hell came into my mouth. It went down my throat, into my stomach, and filled my lungs. I was immersed in a baptism of absolute horror. My eyes felt like they were being consumed out of my sockets. And yet they were still there. My whole body was on fire and burning like a marshmallow dropped into the red coals of a campfire.

I came to the absolute bleak truth that in no way could hell ever be exaggerated. Everything I had ever heard or read about the eternal destiny of the lost and the damned, those who do not love God, does not sufficiently describe what I was experiencing right at that moment. No words could exist to describe the intense pain, the heart wrenching sorrow, the absolute agony, and the everlasting torments of hell. Hell is totally deaf to the cries and agonies of those who are swallowed up and wallowing in its belly.

"And death and hell were cast into the lake of fire. This is the second death. And whosoever was not found written in the book of life was cast into the lake of fire" (Rev. 20:14-15).

Why Forever?

Over and over God has warned humanity about hell. Why? Because He does not want us to go there. He has done everything He can to save, redeem, deliver, rescue, and convert us. God longs to help us, so desperate that He gave His only begotten Son in order to rescue and save us. He took upon Himself our sins, torments, and pains.

"For God so loved the world, that he gave his only begotten Son, that whosoever believeth in him should not perish, but have everlasting life" (John 3:16).

Jesus did not die just to forgive us our sins but to destroy the sinful and selfish nature of the devil that is in our flesh and soul. You see, my friend, God is coming back to take a bride for His Son out from the midst of the wicked human race. It will be a glorious bride absolutely head over heels in love with her groom, which is Jesus Christ. This bride will be made up of people who want to love God and His Son more than anything else. I hope you are part of this church. And if you are not, there is still hope that you can become a part of the body and bride of Christ.

"Who will have all men to be saved, and to come unto the knowledge of truth" (1 Tim. 2:4).

"The Lord is not slack concerning his promise, as some men count slackness; but is longsuffering

to us-ward, not willing that any should perish,
but that all should come to repentance"
(2 Pet. 3:9).

God gave us Jesus in order to give us victory over our filthy, sinful, wicked, self-seeking, self-pleasing, self-centered, self-loving, and self-obsessed lives. Jesus Christ, Emanuel, who is God in the flesh, took upon Himself the sins of the world—your sins and mine. The Creator, Author, and Maker of all things died upon the cross. That is amazing and awesome love. He did this so that we could be free from sin and selfishness from the nature of the devil. Jesus is the only remedy we have from our sinful natures. He is the only antidote from the wrath and anger, and tribulation and anguish of the righteous judgment of a holy God.

You see, a righteous judge must always give a punishment worthy of the crime that was committed. The punishment which is required for the crime reveals the seriousness of that which transpired. The price that Christ had to pay reveals the horrendous seriousness of the situation. And one sin, not covered under the blood, deserves an eternal damnation. Hell, with all of its torments, reveals how deplorable sin really is. It is so wicked that we see that in order for man to be redeemed God had to suffer and die upon the cross for the selfishness of humanity.

How much more do we deserve, seeing that our sins are piled higher than the mountains of this world? But, you might ask, why such a place as hell? First we need to realize that man is an immortal soul, which means that we are eternal. When God created us He made us in His likeness and in His image. We are made of a divine substance. It declares in Genesis that when God breathed into the body of man, he became a living soul.

"So God created man in his own image, in the image of God created he him; male and female created he them" (Gen. 1:27).

"And the LORD God formed man of the dust of the ground, and breathed into his nostrils the breath of life; and man became a living soul" (Gen. 2:7).

We can never enter into a state of nonexistence. Some would have you to believe that we will get a second chance and come back as something or somebody else. These are all the wishes of those who are hoping that they do not have to stand before their maker. But they will have no choice in this matter. Now you might ask if God is love, why would He create such a hideous place called hell and send man there? God knew when He made us what would happen. And He knew beforehand the price that He would have to pay for our redemption.

When Jesus was about to die on the cross for the human race, He asked the Father if there was another way. But there was no other option, there was no other way. It is the same with hell. There is no other option. God had no choice but to create a place where fallen angels, devils, demons, sinners, and selfish people would be locked away forever so that sin never again contaminates and corrupts God's creation. If there could have been any other way, God would have made it.

What many do not realize is that hell is a place where the wicked are quarantined. A good example of why people have to be quarantined can be discovered in the history of the human race. Hundreds of millions have died and are still dying because of infectious diseases when they are not contained. Historically, seven of the most deadly known diseases that mankind has experienced are smallpox, the

Spanish flu, the Black Plague, tuberculosis, malaria, Ebola virus, and cholera. Whole civilizations have been wiped out because they were not able to quarantine these diseases.[3] Hell is God's quarantine, a holding cell for the most deadly disease that ever has or ever will exist. Sin is the very nature of the devil, which was engrafted into the heart and soul of man when he committed sin in the Garden of Eden.

It is true that we need to have a divine revelation of the character and nature of Christ within our hearts. But we also desperately need to have a divine revelation of man's fallen nature. The satanic seed has been underestimated for its deviousness and wicked nature. It is also called the seed of the serpent. The corruptible seed. Just look at the price that was paid for our salvation, and realize how dangerous the satanic seed truly is.

> *"The heart is deceitful above all things, and desperately wicked: who can know it?"*
> *(Jer. 17:9).*

> *"How much more abominable and filthy is man, which drinketh iniquity like water?" (Job 15:16).*

The majority of the twenty-first century church has lost the revelation of the sinfulness of man. Some have even foolishly declared that when a person gives their heart to Christ the old man died automatically. You would have to be absolutely naive to accept this philosophy. Of course it's the enemy of our soul that would propagate such a foolish belief. You would have to deny the obvious to accept this doctrine of demons. It is the wickedness of a man's heart that reveals the answer of why even if a man has never heard of the name of Jesus, he will still go to hell. The seed of the devil wrapped itself around the DNA of man's human flesh when man ate the forbidden fruit of the tree

49

of the knowledge of good and evil in the Garden of Eden. This seed of sin is passed on from generation to generation. The human soul is hung between the flesh and the Spirit. Eventually the soul is overwhelmed by the virus, cancer, and corruptible nature that is in the human flesh. And the soul of man dies.

> *"For the flesh lusteth against the Spirit, and the Spirit against the flesh: and these are contrary the one to the other: so that ye cannot do the things that ye would" Gal. 5:17).*

> *"There is therefore now no condemnation to them which are in Christ Jesus, who walk not after the flesh, but after the Spirit" (Rom. 8:1).*

Swallowed Up in Darkness

Now at that very moment excruciating pain overtook me. It penetrated my mind, and inflamed every fiber of my being. It stuck to my flesh like melted black tar. The lava was like burning mud that sucked me into the very depths of hell. Deeper and deeper I sunk. It pulled me down like a whirlpool. I wish I could be more graphic in how it felt. How deep I sunk I do not know. The depths of the oceans of this present world are nothing in comparison with the depths of hell. For it is called the bottomless pit. I could not resist its current. It pulled and sucked at me like quicksand. I gave up all hope of ever coming to the surface. I was covered and engulfed in total darkness. I could not see anything. Now you understand that my eyes were not burned out of my head. I could still see. And yet I could not see, because there was no light.

The Bible declares that there is no light in hell to be had. There is no light of the sun, the moon, the stars, or even a flame. It is the darkness of eternal midnight. When I began this journey, and throughout it, for the most part I could see what was taking place. God allowed me to see because He wanted me to behold what was happening in the underworld of the lost. For those who are eternally lost in hell this is not normal. They will never see light again because they have rejected the light of Jesus Christ. They will never have the privilege of seeing the glorious lights of creation again.

> *"But the children of the kingdom shall be cast out into utter darkness: there shall be weeping and gnashing of teeth" (Matt. 8:12).*

The darkness of hell is not just a natural darkness. It is a supernatural intense darkness possibly similar to what happened when God poured out His wrath upon Egypt in the days of Moses.

> *"And the LORD said unto Moses, Stretch out thine hand toward heaven, that there may be darkness over the land of Egypt, even darkness which may be felt. And Moses stretched forth his hand toward heaven; and there was a thick darkness in all the land of Egypt three days: They saw not one another, neither rose any from his place for three days: but all the children of Israel had light in their dwellings" (Exod. 10:21-23).*

My friend there is no light in hell, just a maddening, absolutely horrible, frightening, tangible, eternal darkness. All light is extinguished. It is the black realms of misery and of woe. It is the blackness of darkness forever. Can you imagine being sucked up into the burning, bubbling, churning lava of hell? Can you imagine the never-ending, searing pains of eternal damnation and separation where there is no light? Hell is a prison for souls forever lost in darkness of selfishness, forever locked in to the demonic nature of the devil.

Would Not Die

Now, as I was sucked deeper into the lava, brimstone and sulfur, the burning mud of hell was in my mouth, and I could not breathe. My lungs were collapsing. I kept trying to suck in oxygen, but I could not. I was suffocating, and yet, I did not die. My flesh was burning, and yet, I did not die. My brain was being ripped apart from the pain and sensations in my body, and yet, I did not die. The flames of hell were burning my eyes, my tongue, my hands, and my belly from the crown of my head to the soles of my feet, I was in excruciating pain. The burning, boiling, searing, brimstone and sulfur of hell were penetrating every fiber of my being, and yet, I did not die. I am not in the least exaggerating my experience, if anything I am under-rating it.

As I was going through these terrible sensations, I felt an upward thrust pushing me toward the top of the lake of fire. A strong type of current was dragging me a long. And then I came to the surface. I began bobbing up and down as I was being moved along, turning, end over end, head over heels, rolling and tumbling with the swirling masses of those around me in the violent waves and currents of hell. By now, you would think that all of my feelings would have been gone, burned out into nonexistence, that all of my five senses would have been seared into nothingness. You would think that I would have gone into absolute and total shock, that I would have been virtually and completely numb. But that was not the case. Every one of my five senses was still very much alive.

I could touch, taste, hear, smell; I could see the torments of hell. Now I can tell you, my friend, by personal experience that the most extreme and bizarre torments that a person could ever experience on Earth is nothing compared to the never-ending torments of hell.

The Devil

My friends, sin is not the will of God and never was His will. God made man in His image and in His likeness. Man was totally free from selfishness even as God is. There was no pride in man's heart, no arrogance or rebellion. Just the meekness, humility, goodness and love of God were there. He was to rule and to reign with God, to walk at His side forever. He was to be His companion. But when man yielded his soul, his mind, his body, by his own free will to the devil by the partaking of the forbidden fruit of the tree of knowledge of good and evil, the divine DNA of heaven no longer ruled and reigned over his heart. The seed of selfishness was planted into the soil of man's flesh eventually invading the human soul. No longer was he selfless, but he became just like the devil. Selfish! The devil has become natural man's earthly father.

"Ye are of your father the devil, and the lusts of your father ye will do. He was a murderer from the beginning, and abode not in the truth, because there is no truth in him. When he speaketh a lie, he speaketh of his own: for he is a liar, and the father of it" (John 8:44).

Satan became the god of this age!

"In whom the god of this world hath blinded the minds of them which believe not, lest the

53

*light of the glorious gospel of Christ, who is
the image of God, should shine unto them"
(2 Cor. 4:4).*

The devil and all of his demonic entities, fallen
angels, imps, apostate, wicked, lying spirits exist for one
reason and one reason only: to drag your soul and my
soul to hell with them.

*"The theif cometh not, but for to steal, and to
kill, and to destroy: I am come that they may
have life, and that they might have it more
abundantly" (John 10:10).*

Demons endeavor to harden our hearts and blind
our eyes by getting us to act, live, speak, and to walk in
selfishness. This is our will being done.

*"Be sober, the vigilant; because your adversary
the devil, as a roaring lion, walketh about,
seeking whom he may devour" (2 Pet. 5:8).*

Demons may even be coming for your soul as you are
reading this book if you are not right with God. People need
to understand that sin is the very seed and image of the
devil permeating the flesh and eventually the heart of a man.
There must be a change, a conversion and a transformation
in our hearts. We must allow God to give us a new heart.
The human heart is sick. The old sinful nature, selfishness,
must die. It must be crucified. The true believer crucifies the
selfish nature. If we walk in the nature of Jesus Christ we
will not fulfill the lust of the satanic nature.

*"And they that are Christ's have crucified the
flesh with the affections and lusts" (Gal. 5:24).*

54

"For if we have been planted together in the likeness of his death, we shall be also in the likeness of his resurrection" (Rom. 6:5).

The very last enemy to be put under the feet of the believer is his physical body. This corruption will put on corruption.

"So also is the resurrection of the dead. It is sown in corruption; it is raised in incorruption" (I Cor. 15:42).

"For this corruptible must put on incorruption, and this mortal must put on immortality" (I Cor. 15:53).

You might think that if you end up in hell you can turn away from your wicked deeds, but man will not and cannot repent in hell because the character of a sinner cannot be changed once he is dead! If you die a sinner, you will remain a sinner. If you die a saint, you will remain a saint. We will be permanently locked into one of these two natures according to which one we yielded ourselves to before our deaths.

"He that is unjust, let him be unjust still: and he which is filthy, let him be filthy still: and he that is righteous, let him be righteous still: and he that is holy, let him be holy still" (Rev. 22:11).

"If the clouds be full of rain, they empty themselves upon the earth: and if the tree fall toward the south, or toward the north, in the place where the tree falleth, there it shall be" (Eccles. 11:3).

A number of years ago a tragic death happened to a relative I deeply loved. I was tormented with the thought of whether or not they went to hell. In the midst of my torment the Spirit of God spoke to my heart. What is strange is that He did not reveal to me where this particular loved one went. Many people today would love it if God would lie to them and tell them their loved one went to heaven when, in truth, they did not.

What the Lord did speak to my heart was that even if someone I loved ended up in hell, they would not truly be the person that I knew in this life. I asked the Lord in what sense He meant, that they were not the same person. He spoke to me and said, "All of their goodness and kindness, meekness, gentleness, and godly characteristics that you loved were taken away when they died." Even as when a Christian dies, all that was evil and devilish is permanently stripped and purged from them, never more to be experienced or realized. All that was evil is removed from their hearts and their lives forever. Do not misunderstand what is being said here. That person who is in heaven or in hell is still the same soul. But all that was evil is removed. Or all that was good and holy is removed. They are either like the angels in heaven, or they are like the devils and demons in hell. Heaven and all of its citizens are absolutely and completely holy and pure.

Please listen to me, God will never allow sin and selfishness to run loose in His creation again. It would corrupt, pollute, and destroy all that God has created. It is the absolute opposite of all that God is. God is light; sin is darkness. God is selfless; sin is selfishness. God is absolutely pure and good. Sin is absolute filth and evil. God is love. Sin is the hate of God. It is the heart shouting and declaring *my will be done!*

> *"Let no man say when he is tempted, I am tempted of God: for God cannot be tempted with*

evil, neither tempteth he any man: But every man is tempted, when he is drawn away of his own lust, and enticed. Then when lust hath conceived, it bringeth forth sin: and sin, when it is finished, bringeth forth death. Do not err, my beloved brethren. Every good gift and every perfect gift is from above, and cometh down from the Father of lights, with whom is no variableness, neither shadow of turning" (James 1:13-17).

Sin is absolute pure evil. Look at what sin has done to humanity! All of the wars, death, famines, disease, sickness, crimes, hate and strife, divorce, addictions, poverty, hunger, and pain is because of sin. It is selfishness that is infused into the flesh of man and eventually into the heart and soul of man.

Many people today absolutely believe and confess that they are Christians. They think they are saved. They believe that they are going to heaven. But they do not love and obey or follow God. They will not do the will God. But he that would go to heaven when he dies must walk the way of holiness and love while he lives. For the Bible declares that without holiness and without love no man will see God.

"If any man love not the Lord Jesus Christ, let him be Anathema Maranatha [eternally damned]" (1Cor. 16:22).

" If ye love me, keep my commandments" (John 14:15).

"For this is the love of God, that we keep his commandments: and his commandments are not greivous" (1 John 5:3).

The person who will not come out of his selfishness, will be eternally separated from God. It is ridiculous and insane to think that you are going to heaven with willful sin and rebellion still in your heart against God and His Word. The major difference between the saved and the unsaved is that those who are going to heaven have made it their ultimate purpose in life to love God with all of their hearts, souls, minds, and with all their strength and being. They also purpose to love their neighbors as themselves. If we have rejected the truth, then we have rejected God's will for our lives. If we rejected His holiness and if we have rejected His Word, then we have rejected the very character and nature of Christ, who gives us victory over selfishness, sin, and darkness. Then God has no choice but to reject us!

> *"I am come a light into the world, that whosoever believeth on me should not abide in darkeness"* *(John 12:46).*

> *"For every one that doeth evil hateth the light, lest his deeds should be reproved" (John 3:20).*

The truth of the matter is that the old man must be crucified. If we do not mortify the flesh, we will be cast into outer darkness. Over and over the New Testament teaches that we must walk in the new nature. We must put on the new man and make no provision to fulfill the lusts thereof. The grace of God is the divine nature of Christ and His ability to overcome sin within us. Literally grace is the power of God to overcome sin. If we do not surrender to God's divine nature, we will be damned, and we will be forever doomed. We will be eternally lost. There is no reason why that should happen. Christ has already paid the ultimate price for our salvation. We simply need to believe it and then walk in the nature of Christ.

58

"For by grace are ye saved through faith; and that not of yourselves: it is the gift of God: Not of works, lest any man should boast. For we are his workmanship, created in Christ Jesus unto good works, which God hath before ordained that we should walk in them" (Eph. 2:8-10).

Worms

In hell there is a worm. It is the worm of your memory, the anguish of your soul, the worm of your conscience. It is the thought of lost happiness and lost opportunities to get right with God. The worm is the reality of the fact that you heard this message—you heard this truth—but you did not believe it. You read the Bible, but you did not live it. You could have walked with God, but you did not. And now your memory will eat away at you forever. Your memory will devour you from the inside out and yet never cease to exist. Oh, how terrible! In hell there are untold billions of husbands and wives, fathers and mothers, sons and daughters, hopelessly lost forever swallowed up in the fires of hell, gnawed by the worm that never dies.

The Scriptures also imply that in hell there is another kind of worm. In my fictitious book called the *Chronicles of Micah,* I reveal an experience that Micah had in hell with worms. As Micah was pulled along in the lake of fire, he noticed that there were some other creatures in this boiling molasses of pain. They looked like some kind of large, extremely ugly, terrifying worms. They would come to the surface then disappear, then return to the surface and disappear again. It was as if they were searching and hungering for something. Or was it somebody? It sent chills up and down his spine, even though he was in excruciating pain. Unconsciously he found himself trying to hide from them. But he could not run or hide. About twenty feet away from him, a number of these large ugly worms broke the surface then disappeared, broke the surface then disappeared, and broke the surface again. Then he noticed that they were coming straight toward him.

In less than ten seconds, they were upon him. Not only were they upon him, but they were digging their way into him. They pushed their way into his already hurting, burning flesh. They squirmed and pushed and wiggled their way into his body. He could feel them crawling inside of him. Absolute disgust and dismay filled his heart and mind as they explored every fiber of his being. They even pushed their way up his throat and into his brain. They would either squirm out of his ears, or they would push their way past his eyes, coming out of the sockets, only to enter back into him somewhere else. He couldn't get them out, and he couldn't stop them. They were driving him insane.

"Thy pomp is brought down to the grave, and the noise of thy viols: the worm is spread under thee, and the worms cover thee" (Isa. 14:1).

"And they shall go forth, and look upon the carcases of the men that have transgressed against me: for their worm shall not die, neither shall their fire be quenched; and they shall be an abhorring unto all flesh" (Isa. 66:24).

Jesus made the same statement about the worm in Mark 9:44, 46 and 48; *"Where their worm dieth not, and the fire is not quenched."*

Chapter 6
Eternity

There seemed to be no end to this nightmare called hell. A second dragged into an hour. A minute turned into a year, and an hour became an everlasting eternity. This was just the beginning of forever. There is no end to this place called hell. There is no escape. There is no exit. There is no way out. Hell is eternal; it is forever. Some would have you believe otherwise. You and I both know without a shadow of a doubt that God is eternal.

"For I am the LORD, I change not" (Mal. 3:6a).

"Jesus Christ the same yesterday, and today, and forever" (Heb. 13:8).

His Word is eternal; heaven and earth shall pass away. If God is everlasting, His Word is everlasting, and heaven is everlasting. Then so is the wrath, the anger, and the judgment of God everlasting.

"And the smoke of their torment ascendeth up for ever and ever: and they have no rest day or night" (Rev. 14:11).

Some believe that when Christ died upon the cross that the sacrifice that Jesus made changed the Father. But that is an utter and horrendous lie. What Christ did on the cross was never meant to change God the Father. For God does not need to be changed.

> *"Every good gift and every perfect gift is from above, and cometh down from the Father of lights, with whom is no variableness, neither shadow of turning" (James 1:17).*

But Jesus' death on the cross was meant to change you and me. Have you ever stopped to think who spoke hell into existence? Who created hell? The Scriptures clearly declare that everything that was created was created by Jesus Christ. You heard correctly, the Scriptures clearly declare that God the Father created all things by the hands of Jesus.

> *"All things were made by him; and without him was not any thing made that was made"*
> *(John 1:3).*

> *"For by him were all things created, that are in heaven, and that are in earth, visible and invisible, whether they be thrones, or dominions, or principalities, or powers: all things were created by him, and for him: And he is before all things, and by him all things consist"*
> *(Col 1:16-17).*

Our blessed Savior and Redeemer, He who shed His precious blood for our redemption, gave His life and gave His all for humanity, brought hell into existence. Therefore hell must need to exist for the safety and good of all creation. Hell was not created for man but for the devil and his angels. Jesus longs to rescue the human race from this terrible and horrible place.

Glimpse of Forever

Now, imagine if you could for just a moment that the earth was made up of nothing but grains of sand. Now imagine that God gave to a pigeon the job of grabbing one grain of sand at a time to fly that grain of sand to the other side of the universe. Then the pigeon is to come all the way back to get another grain of sand and do the same thing. It would take billions of trillions of years for just one round trip. The known universe is at least 150 million light-years wide. The speed of light is approximately 186,000 miles per second. One light year would be 6,000,000,000,000 miles. By the time that pigeon removes the whole Earth to the other side of the universe, eternity is not in the middle; it is not at the end. It is just at the beginning. The suffering and torment in hell will never cease. The fires of hell will never go out. For it is fueled by the bodies of fallen humanity and demonic angels that will never burn up. And when you have been there the space of as many years as there are stars in the heavens, as many leaves on the trees, as the sand on the seashore, eternity will have just begun. A minute in hell will seem longer than a whole life of misery on the earth. We need to ask ourselves if the short-lived, momentary pleasures, the selfishness of physical fulfillment of this life is worth selling our hearts and souls for, knowing that we will spend a never-ending eternity in everlasting torment for meaningless and vain enjoyments. Our souls are composed of immortal substance. All of the human race was created as the offspring of God. For us to cease to exist, God would have to cease to exist. And this will never be.

"For in him we live, and move, and have our being; as certain also of your own poets have said, For we are also his offspring"
(Acts 17:28).

> *"Before the mountains were brought forth, or ever thou hadst formed the earth and the world, even from everlasting to everlasting, thou art God" (Ps. 90:2).*

Another distressing reality that came to me is that in this place called hell there is no relief. There is nowhere you can go in hell to get relief. For how long? Forever! When will it end? Never! Are we ready to pay this terrible price for momentary pleasures, for sin? Esau, the brother of Jacob, gave up his inheritance for a bowl of porridge. Please don't give up heaven. Please don't give up walking with God. Please don't give up eternity with Jesus for a life of selfishness in this world. Those in hell right now would go through anything, suffer any pains to get out of hell. But it is too late for them.

> *"For ye know how that afterward, when he would have inherited the blessing, he was rejected: for he found no place of repentance, though he sought it carefully with tears" (Heb. 12:17).*

Satan and Hell

Within the church many have been taught that the souls of the damned are tormented in hell by demons, devils and imps. There are also many stories of people who were upon the bed of death or who literally died and were tormented by devils, demons, and imps as they were descending to hell. First let me declare that in my experience I did not see demons, devils, imps or fallen angels tormenting people. I think this particular area must be specifically spoken to for a number of reasons.

There is much misunderstanding when it comes to what is going on in the underworld. I'm referring to hell. There are those who have died as sinners and came back to share the horrors of what happened to them from the other side of death. By Scripture, I am totally convinced if you die a sinner, that the demonic powers of the satanic realm are there at your death to meet you. They gladly and fervently take a hold of you and torment you. They mock you and attack you as your soul falls into the deep, dark depths; the bottomless pit of eternal damnation. When I had my experience none of the demonic host were there to meet me or torment me for two main reasons. Number one, I was not dying. Number two, my heart was right with God. I was in love with Jesus and walking in His will.

Jesus declared that the prince of this world was coming to see Him. But that there was not anything in Him that gave the enemy purchase or authority over Him.

"Hereafter I will not talk much with you: for the prince of this world cometh, and hath nothing in me" (John 14:30).

And yet the Scriptures imply that there were demonic powers present at the crucifixion and death of Jesus Christ because He was made to be sin for us.

"For dogs have compassed me: the assembly of the wicked have inclosed me: they pierced my hands and my feet" (Ps. 22:16).

As those who love and follow Christ, we have been delivered from the powers of darkness. We no longer belong to him because we are walking in the reality of the new nature. We are following, loving, and serving God. I have not proclaimed a sinless life. For only Jesus was sinless. But we are pressing in and living a life of continual repentance, confessing our sins when we do miss God's will, trusting God to give is victory over all known sin.

Now we know biblically that some of the angels that had followed Lucifer are chained and locked up in the darkness of hell. The Scriptures do not declare that God locked up all of the spirits that followed Lucifer. For Scripture implies there were numbers beyond count.

> *"For if God spared not the angels that sinned, but cast them down to hell, and delivered them into chains of darkness, to be reserved unto judgment" (2 Pet. 2:4).*

According to the Scriptures there are four angels that are in chains under the Euphrates River, and they will kill a third of the population of the earth at the time of their release.

> *"Saying to the sixth angel which had the trumpet, Loose the four angels which are bound in the great river Euphrates. And the four angels were loosed, which were prepared for an hour, and a day, and a month, and a year, for to slay the third part of men" (Rev. 9:14-15).*

Hell is not a place where demons have the pleasure of tormenting people. This is not just my opinion. When Jesus Christ was here in His earthly ministry the demons were constantly crying out begging Him not to torment them before their time. They even asked Him not to cast them into the deep.

> *"And, behold, they cried out, saying, What have we to do with thee, Jesus, thou Son of God? art thou come hither to torment us before the time?" (Matt. 8:29).*

> *"Then shall he say also unto them on the left hand, Depart from me, ye cursed, into everlasting fire, prepared for the devil and his angels" (Matt. 25:41).*

66

Beloved, demons, imps, devils, and fallen angels are not tormenting people in hell. One time I was in prayer and asked the Lord what this was all about. People are teaching that the satanic world is tormenting people in the place of everlasting torment. The Spirit of the Lord spoke to me and told me that the devil and wicked, evil spirits are constantly trying to exalt and glorify themselves. It gives the enemy great pleasure to convince people it is him and his hoard that humanity needs to fear. By believing that it is demons that torment people in hell, it takes away from the fear of the Lord. It is the wrath and anger, judgment and vengeance of Almighty God that men need to fear—not the devil. The beginning of wisdom is the fear of the Lord. It is not the fear of being tormented by demons throughout eternity.

"It is a fearful thing to fall into the hands of the living God" (Heb. 10:31).

"And fear not them which kill the body, but are not able to kill the soul: but rather fear HIM which is able to destroy both soul and body in hell" (Matt. 10:28).

The enemy has used Greek mythology and those who would propagate the doctrine of purgatory to spread this belief. Please listen to me, God is not using devils, demons, imps, and fallen angels in hell to torment people. It is a place where they themselves are tormented. If you look at how they responded when Jesus confronted them, it is obvious that hell is the last place they want to be. They are absolutely terrified and horrified of hell, even as we should be.

Hell has sufficient pain and agony without God having to use fallen rebellious spirits. Believing this reveals to a great extent that those who propagated this theology really do not understand what the pains and the sufferings of hell are all about. (I will try to answer that question a little later.)

But wasn't it in hell where Jesus defeated the enemy you might ask? No beloved! Jesus did not defeat the devil and the demonic host in hell. Hell is not the devil's domain. In His sufferings upon the cross, in His death, resurrection, and ascension, Christ defeated the devil and the demonic host. Please study the following Scriptures. They clearly reveal this truth.

> *"And having spoiled principalities and powers, he made a shew of them openly, triumphing over them in it"* *(Col. 2:15).*

> *"For we wrestle not against flesh and blood, but against principalities, against powers, against the rulers of the darkness of this world, against spiritual wickedness in high places"* *(Eph. 6:12).*

The Last Words of Sinners

I have included here true testimonies of last words of sinners that are documented by the Reverend S. B. Shaw in his book *The Dying Testimonies of Saved and Unsaved.* This book was first published in 1898 and can now be found in its entirety on the Internet. [4]

The Death of John

John was a young man who rejected the Gospel. As he was upon his deathbed, this is what he cried out:

"O mother! mother, get me some water to quench this fire that is burning me to death"; then he tore his hair and rent his breast; the fire had already begun to burn, the smoke of which shall ascend up forever and ever. And then again he cried, "O mother, save me, the devils have come after me. O mother, take

Eternity

me in your arms, and don't let them have me." And as his mother drew near to him, he buried his face in that fond bosom which had nourished and cherished him,...he turned from her and with an unearthly voice he shrieked, "Father! Mother! Father, save me; they come to drag my soul—my soul to hell." And with his eyes starting from their sockets, he fell back upon his bed a corpse. [5]

Death of William Pope

Even as Mr. Pope was dying he stated that he had no desire to receive God's blessing. Here is his story:
And then [he] cried out, 'Oh, the hell, the torment, the fire that I feel within me! Oh, eternity! eternity! To dwell forever with devils and damned spirits in the burning lake must be my portion, and that justly!'...'Oh the burning flame, the hell, the pain I feel!... – in the lake which burns with fire and brimstone!'...The day he died, when Mr. Rhodes visited with him, and asked the privilege to pray once more with him, he cried out with great strength, considering his weakness, "No!" and passed away in the evening without God. [6]

Death of Jennie G.

This woman was under deep conviction for sin at a revival, but refused to get right with God. Later she fell deathly ill, and on her deathbed she cried out:

"The fiends, they come; O save me! They drag me down! Lost! lost! lost! she whispered as she struggled in the agonies of death..."Bind me, ye chains of darkness! Oh! that I might cease to be, but still exist. The worm that never dies, the second death." [And at that] Jennie G. lay a lifeless form of clay. [7]

Death of Mr. W

Mr. W. died in 1883 and was an avowed infidel. As he neared death Mr. W. cried out:

"O God, deliver me from that awful pit!...I am in the flames—pull me out, pull me out!" He kept repeating this until the breath left his body. As the bodily strength failed his words became more faint....his departing whispers...were, "Pull me out, pull me out!" [8]

Death of an Old Man

There was an old man said to be "an aged and rebellious infedel." Here is his story:

Shortly before he died he started suddenly up in his bed, screaming, "The devils are come, the devils are come, keep them off me!" and then fell into a swoon. Just before he died he seemed to summon all his strength, rose up in his bed, shouted "Hell and damnation, hell and damnation!" fell back, choked, strangled and died. [9]

Death of Josie

As Josie was upon her deathbed she began to in a low tone:

"It must be done! It must be done!" Continuing to repeat the same with increasing force and higher pitch of voice, until she would end with a piercing scream, "It must be done!" Her husband asked her, "Josie, what must be done?" She answered, "Our hearts must be made right!" And again she would entreat me to take her away, affirming she could see devils all around her. She would say, "See them laugh!" [10]

Apparently, she experienced more hideous events before she finally breathes her last. And as far as we know she did not believe on Christ but went to hell.

Death of Miss A.

This is the story of Miss A. who lived in Georgia:

Miss A....was taken very sick, and was informed that she could not live....she said "Oh, the devil is coming to drag my soul down to hell! Don't live in pleasure and be found wanting, but live in Christ complete and wanting nothing. I am lost, lost forever! Oh, lost, lost, lost!"—then died. [11]

Death of a Young Man

This is the story of a young man who was ill:

He was taken ill, and during his sickness he would exclaim, "Oh, drive these Devils away with their chains, they would drag my soul down to hell before I die! Oh, brother and sister, take warning! Don't come to this hell. This is hell enough! The devils are dragging me down!" And as he cried mightily, "Don't come to this hell of woe, this hell, this hell!" his soul departed to everlasting ruin and perdition. [12]

Allow me to clarify that these devils and demons which were present at the death of these sinners were not there to torment them in hell. But they were there in order to torment them as they were going to hell, to gloat and laugh at the pain and the suffering which was awaiting them. They were also present to convince them that there was no hope for them to be saved. They whispered and lied to their minds that salvation and repentance was beyond their grasp. It is so sad that they listened to the voices of these demented and the fallen spirits. Even now many in our society and present world still listen to lies and deceptions of the demonic world.

> *"The harvest is past, the summer is ended, and we are not saved" (Jer. 8:20).*

From all accounts and testimonies, there seems to be a brief period at the death of a sinner before the lost soul enters into hell. In this time period, demonic powers torment and afflict the sinner. In all of my research on this particular subject, there is testimony after testimony of sinners dying and being tormented *before* they end up in hell. Maybe this is where the philosophy of Purgatory came from. As far as I can determine, until the soul reaches the Lake of fire (hell), there is the possibility of being raised from the dead. It is in this moment of time where people cry out to God for another chance, and God in his mercy and grace rescues them. Even well known Christian people such as Kenneth E. Hagen have had this type of experience.[13]

Chapter 7
No Love

If you can imagine in the midst of the pain and agony, another even much greater and terrifying torment began to flood my soul. It was emotional, spiritual, psychological, and mental. Here in this place, this bubbling, boiling slime pit called hell, there is absolutely no love. It is totally void of all love. Even when I was a sinner, I was surrounded by the love of God, His goodness, provision, and blessings. I may not have recognized or even realized it. Whether I knew it or not, God was watching over me. He was protecting, helping, and reaching out to me, even though I was not serving Him or loving Him. A guardian angel was there all the time, though I could not see him. Jesus said:

> *"Take heed that ye despise not one of these little ones; for I say unto you, That in heaven their angels do always behold the face of my Father which is in heaven"* *(Matt. 18:10).*

Nature, birds, animals, and all of creation display the unfathomable love of God. The shining sun, the green grass, the budding flowers, the blue gray waters of the sea, the light blue skies, the glowing moon, and the sparkling stars at night. They all declare God's awesome love for His creation. The beautiful fragrances that float upon the wind and the singing birds with their beautiful songs declare His love. God has blessed us and revealed Himself to us by His awesome creation according to Scriptures on God's goodness.

> *"Or despisest thou the riches of his goodness and forbearance and longsuffering; not knowing that the goodness of God leadeth thee to repentance?" (Rom. 2:4).*

> *"That ye may be the children of your Father which is in heaven: for he maketh his sun to rise on the evil and on the good, and sendeth rain on the just and on the unjust" (Matt. 5:45).*

We need to understand that unconverted, unregenerated man has accepted and believed the lies of evolution. But it is a lie from the satanic realm.

> *"In whom the god of this world hath blinded the minds of them which believe not, lest the light of the glorious gospel of Christ, who is the image of God, should shine unto them"*
> *(2 Cor. 4:4).*

For God is the Author, Creator, Maker, Architect and Master Designer of all of creation. God gave us the breath we are breathing, the clothes we are wearing, the food we are eating, the body we are living in; it all comes from God. He gave us all of the talents and abilities we have in order to put within our hands these possessions. All that we have that is good and beautiful, lovely and beneficial, comes from God. It is God's divine marriage proposal, a divine romance. For you see, God is calling, pleading, imploring, and asking us to follow Him into light everlasting.

"Behold, I stand at the door, and knock: if any man hear my voice, and open the door, I will come in to him, and will sup with him, and he with me" (Rev. 3:20).

*"We love him, because he first loved us."
(1 John 4:19).*

Jesus paid the ultimate price for the hand of His bride. He bought us with every drop of His precious blood in His body. And He longs for us to follow Him down the wedding aisle to the throne of His Father, to be one with Him forever. You see, my friend, God is striving to lead us to a place of turning our backs upon our selfish lives, to crucify and mortify the corruptible and damnable seed of selfishness, which is the very nature of the devil and his fallen angels—the demonic horde. We must believe on the Lord Jesus Christ. We must walk in His divine nature of love so that we can be one with Him forever.

"Every good gift and perfect gift is from above, and cometh down from the Father of lights, with whom is no variableness, neither shadow of turning" (James 1:17).

Are you taking carelessly God's abundant goodness, His kindness, His patience, and the fact that He has suffered a long time waiting for you? Do you not grasp that His kindness is meant to cause you to turn away from selfishness?

Our number one desire should be to love Him with all of our hearts. True Christianity is simply striving to love God with all of your heart, spirit, soul, mind, and body. We love Him because He first loved us. Love our neighbors as we love ourselves. We need to respond to His amazing love.

All of creation will be our jury, and they will declare us guilty of the most perverse wickedness and corruption if we do not. To think that we would turn down such a wonderful and awesome gift from God is unfathomable. The reality is that Jesus is offering us to be made one with Himself simply by acknowledging our wickedness and by forsaking all in order to follow him. Yielding to the divine grace of His nature within us. While we have an opportunity, we need to respond to His unspeakable and amazing love.

But in that God-forsaken, burning slime pit called hell there is no love whatsoever. The goodness of God, the long-sufferings of God, the kindness of God, the blessings of God, and the mercies of God are all gone, eternally lost because people refused to listen. Masses have refused to obey. Multitudes have refused to love Him, even though He invited them to be His bride, His beloved companion for eternity.

All Alone

A loneliness and emptiness beyond description descended upon me. Even though I bumped into many others, there was no communication. You have no recognition of friends and relatives. Those in hell are tormented devils and souls. They are filled with dreadful shrieks, screams caused by the fierceness of their pains. There are fearful blasphemies against God's power and justice who keeps them there. The torments of fellow sufferers do nothing to relieve you of your miseries. It only increases them. And every soul that you lead into hell with you will only magnify your sorrows a hundredfold. Dad and mom, pastor and preacher, teacher and politician, Can you live with yourself knowing your taking some you love to hell with you?

There are many who think that hell will be party time. They laugh, they mock, and they scoff at the reality of hell. They laugh at them who tell them of a place called hell. Their destruction is their own fault, and they will never forget it. And in life they refused to be one with God in order to continue to be one with the world. In hell they are all alone forever. Just this thought should cause us to turn from our selfish ways.

> *"But be ye doers of the word, and not hearers only, deceiving your own selves" (James 1:22).*

You went to church, but did You live the life of a Christian? You said you loved God, but you never loved God. You loved the world; you loved sin. You loved immorality, and you loved perverse and vain amusements.

> *"Love not the world, neither the things that are in the world. If any man love the world, the love of the Father is not in him" (1 John 2:15).*

You rejected the truth. You rejected holiness. You rejected righteousness, and you rejected purity. You rejected God's Word, God's truth, the light, and His cross. You would not die to the world, the flesh, or the devil. You didn't seek God. You didn't obey Him, and you refused to follow Him.

> *"In flaming fire taking vengeance on them that know not God, and that obey not the gospel of our Lord Jesus Christ" (2 Thess. 1:8).*

You loved everything else but God. And because you have rejected God, now God has rejected you. You have forever lost the presence of God. You have lost heaven in all of its glory. You have lost all that is good, holy, and decent. You have lost all of your loved ones. And in hell there is no help, no relief, no escape, and no hope. Forever and ever, there is nothing but torment. I pray and hope to God that this is not a description of your condition. If it is please repent and cry out to God. Trust that Jesus Christ will change your heart, mind, and purpose.

No Water

A thirst took a hold of me, a thirst so intense and so maddening, I thought I would lose my mind. If only I could have just one drop of water, just enough to wet my lips. My need for water became all consuming. But there was none to be had. Hell is a lake that burns with fire and brimstone, but not one drop of water. There is no water in hell. I believe that water is symbolic of God's goodness, kindness, love, mercy, long suffering, and patience. Over 80 percent of the earth is made up of water found in oceans, lakes, seas, rivers, and ponds. We can drink it, bathe in it, swim in it, and we can even drown in it. But once we die, it is too late. Salvation is available now. Jesus tells the story of the rich man and Lazarus:

> *"There was a rich man who used to dressed in fancy clothes and who ate very well every day. There was also a very poor man by the name of Lazarus who was homeless and sick. He was nothing but a mass sores and ulcers. He laid at the gate of the rich man, begging him for the scraps of food that fell off of his table onto the floor. Even the dogs, as they would come by, licked the sores of the poor man. In the course of time, Lazarus died and was carried by angels into Paradise to be with Abraham. The rich man died too and was buried. In hell, the rich man in torment lifted up his eyes. He saw Abraham*

at a distance with Lazarus at his side. So he called to Abraham and said, 'Please have pity on me, and send Lazarus with some water on his finger to cool my tongue; for I am in great agony and pain here in this fire.' But Abraham replied, 'Son, remember that in your lifetime you had tremendous blessings. But Lazarus experienced nothing but troubles and problems. And now it is his turn to be blessed, while it is your turn to be in pain, and agony. And this is not the only reason. Between you and us there is a great chasm. And we cannot get to you, and you cannot get to us.' Then the man said, 'Please, father Abraham, send Lazarus back from the dead to my father's house. For I have five brothers, and I want him to strongly warn them and to tell them the whole truth so that they will not come into this place of suffering, pain, and misery.' But Abraham said to him, 'They have the writings of Moses and the Prophets. Let them read their writings.' And the rich man said, 'No, father Abraham, they won't believe what they read. But if a messenger came to them from the grave, they would completely change.' And Abraham said, 'If they do not listen to Moses and the Prophets, they will not be convinced by someone who has been raised from the dead.'" (See Luke 16:19-31.)

Even as the rich man did not lose his desire for water, those in hell do not lose any of their natural desires, physical, emotional, or psychological. If you go to hell, you'll continue to desire everything you had in your earthly life. All of your cravings and all of the addictions will still be with you, whether it be alcohol or tobacco. It could be drugs or immoral relationships. You will still have all your natural and immoral cravings and longings. You'll want these cravings and desires to end with everything inside of you. But they will never end. It'll never stop. It will just keep on going.

Please, listen to me. This book could be an answer to someone's prayers for you, someone who knows you and is pleading for your soul. And if you reject this message, throughout eternity you will be screaming and crying, begging and pleading for water and all of your other desires. The rich man cried out for water, but it was too late. And you will be tormented forever with both natural and sinful, unfulfilled desires. Your natural and spiritual selfish thirst will never be fulfilled, never satisfied. Your thirsts will never be quenched, and the agony of it will never end.

Endless Pain

In hell there is no relief, no freedom from pain. One's body does not go numb; rather, the pain intensifies. Every part of the soul, body, mind, emotions, and our total being is tormented at once. The human body is a wonderful and marvelous creation.

> *"I will praise thee; for I am fearfully and wonderfully made: marvelous are thy works; and that my soul knoweth right well"*
> *(Ps. 139:14).*

And yet, amazingly the soul of man also has a body. The natural eye cannot see the body of the soul, but that does not mean it does not exist. Your soul in this life looks exactly like your physical body. But in heaven, if you die in Christ, you will receive a glorified body, a body that is glorious and amazing. There'll be no natural blood that flows through your new body. But the very Spirit of God Himself flows through your veins. We will never need sleep. This new body can endure any kind of harshness or atmosphere or environment. It will be absolutely indestructible, eternal, and immortal. According to the Scriptures the unrepentant sinner Himself shall also receive a new body. This body will be cast into the lake of fire with the devil and his angels (see John 5:28-29, 1 Thes. 4:16, and Dan. 12:2).

The body of the soul in this life is very similar to the physical body. The physical body has more nerve endings than what the medical world can scientifically count. All over our bodies we have nerve endings that give us information about the things we touch and experience. For instance, each square inch of the skin in the human body contains more than one thousand nerve endings. The brain alone is estimated to contain more than 100 billion nerve cells. Based upon medical studies, these brain signals travel on the nerves at approximately 225 mph, going from your brain to your toes in less than 1/50 of a second.[14] I believe that the body of the soul is much more sophisticated and sensitive than the physical body. That's one possible reason why when I experienced hell and heaven, everything seemed to me to be much more real. Maybe that's why Paul said when he had his experience he did not know if he was in the body or out of the body.

"I knew a man in Christ above fourteen years ago, (whether in the body, I cannot tell; or whether out of the body, I cannot tell: God knoweth;) such an one caught up to the third heaven" (2 Cor. 12:2).

Throughout the Old and New Testaments you see people having experience after experience with the divine realm. And their descriptions make it seem as if it were physical and real to them. If we look in the book of James chapter two, we would discover a dynamic truth.

> *"For as the body without the spirit is dead, so faith without works is dead also" (James 2:26).*

I believe it is the soul that God takes into the realm of the Spirit to reveal the divine mysteries of the kingdom. It is what the Scripture declares "being in the Spirit."

> *"I was in the Spirit on the Lord's day" (Rev. 1:10a).*

> *"Afterwards the spirit took me up, and brought me in a vision by the Spirit of God into Chaldea, to them of the captivity. So the vision that I had seen went up from me" (Ezek. 11:24).*

Our soul has eyes and ears and all of the same parts as our physical body. But it is far more superior and sensitive than the physical. For the soul is the real us.

In hell, the eyes of our souls are tormented. The ears of our souls are tormented with loud screams, with the continual cries of the damned. The nostrils of are souls are smothered with the overwhelming stench of hell. The body of the soul is forever burned in the liquid fire, and all the realms of our souls are tormented. Our understanding will never leave us alone to the fact that we have lost heaven. We will never lose the understanding that we had so many opportunities of being saved. Our minds are tormented considering how we wasted our precious time, how we missed opportunity after opportunity to get right with God. Our memories and imaginations are tormented in the thoughts of our past pleasures, present pains, and future sorrows. All of this lasts forever. Our conscience is tormented with the continual gnawing worm. An unquenchable fire burns us. The brimstone chokes us. Utter darkness frightens us. The eternal chain ties us.

But why the endless pain? This is a very important question that absolutely needs answering. Is it because God is sadistic? Because He enjoys the pains and sufferings of His creation? No, beloved! It is because of the nature of sin, the very seed of the devil that has penetrated the heart and soul of man. God cannot and must not allow sin to continue. But because the sinner will go on forever how is He going to stop the sinner from sinning? It may seem simplistic, but it really is not.

Here's the answer: Has your mind ever been preoccupied with a thought or an idea while you were doing physical work? For instance, have you ever been pounding nails into a board while your mind was somewhere else? Maybe your mind was upon some thought, ideal, or desire. And then out of the blue you slam your thumb with the hammer. At that very moment all of your thoughts, ideals, and emotions are directed like a laser beam right at the pain in your thumb. Nothing else matters at the time but the pain in your thumb. There's no conniving, plotting, or planning of anything evil. All of the images, dreams, thoughts of wickedness, except for possibly words of certain negative characteristics, are instantly stopped. You are swallowed up in that pain. Simply put, that is exactly what the pain and torment in hell is all about. It is to stop the wicked heart from continuing in its sin. Those who are there may continue in their rant and raves against God, but they cannot plot, connive, and meditate upon the wicked thoughts or imaginations. God must put an end to the sinful shenanigans of the satanic nature. The pain, suffering, agony, and torment of eternal damnation restrain and hinder the satanic nature. But it cannot cleanse the human heart, soul, mind, will, and emotions from the seed of sin. Only through the sacrificial work of Jesus Christ and loving Him can our hearts be cleansed from this dreadful seed of sin.

How long I had been in hell, I do not know. It seemed like an eternity. I had been crying out in pain and agony unconsciously, screaming and wailing like the rest of the damned. And yet my cries were of a totally different nature. Their cries were cursing, profanity, wickedness, begging, and promises of repentance if given another chance. Curses were only to be followed by more curses. The realm of hell is filled with the noise of the damned, weeping and wailing and crying. They were shouting and screaming and yelling and moaning in terrible overwhelming pain. And yet those who are in hell now understand their spiritual condition and that their punishment is just and proper. They understand that they alone are to blame for their present situation and eternal damnation.

You see, my friend, if you die in your sins, all of your riches will be taken away. And you will never buy and sell, get gain anymore, purchase houses or lands. All you will ever have is everlasting shame and contempt. You will no longer have singing or dancing, the sound of music, and no more sweet food. You will be stripped of everything. You will be denied admission into the kingdom of heaven. You will see all the saints of all the ages shine like the sun throughout eternity. When you are weeping, they will be laughing. When you are mourning, they will be glad. When you are crying and howling, they will be leaping and dancing. Sinners, what will you do? The broad, wide way of selfishness and the pleasures of the flesh and sin are for a season. Then you will pay with everlasting suffering, anguish, pain, misery, and sorrow forever.

Cry of Help

Now my cries were to God, justifying, praising, worshiping, and acknowledging that from God came my help. I remember screaming in pain that God is righteous in

84

His judgments and that He is true and faithful and worthy of all glory and honor. From my heart and soul, out of my mouth came a nonstop flow of love and devotion, praise and worship to the Three in One. It might be hard to believe that someone filled with such overwhelming pain and agony could be worshiping and praising the One who was causing such horrible afflictions, and yet that's what I was doing. The Scriptures declare for out of the abundance of the heart the mouth speaks. Then from somewhere within I cried out for deliverance.

"Though he slay me, yet will I trust in him: but I will maintain mine own ways before him" *(Job 13:15).*

"A good man out of the good treasure of his heart bringeth forth that which is good; and an evil man out of the evil treasure of his heart bringeth forth that which is evil: for of the abundance of the heart his mouth speaketh. And why call ye me, Lord, Lord, and do not the things which I say?" (Luke 6:45-46).

God Heard

In the midst of my prayers, I heard a voice that seemed to come from heaven. It was A majestic thunderous and awesome sound. This voice completely overwhelmed all of the sensations I was experiencing at that moment. It literally grabbed hold of me and placed me in a protective bubble. All of my blistered and burning flesh was instantly healed and made whole. My hair, clothes, and body were returned to their original condition just as they were before my journey began. The love and goodness of God came rushing back in to my heart and mind.

The sorrows and woes of hell disappeared. This voice had an amazing effect upon hell. It shook the very foundations of the lake of fire itself. I heard the audible voice of God say, " Let My servant go." The bowels of hell twisted and turned as if in torment. They ripped apart like the Red Sea must have when Moses stretched forth his rod. Hell had no choice but to obey the voice of the Lord of heaven, earth, and hell.

"And said, I cried by reason of my affliction unto the LORD, and he heard me; out of the belly of hell cried I, and thou heardest my voice" (Jonah 2:2).

"The sorrows of hell compassed me about; the snares of death prevented me; In my distress I called upon the LORD, and cried to my God: and he did hear my voice out of his temple, and my cry did enter into his ears. Then the earth shook and trembled; the foundations of heaven moved and shook, because he was wroth. There went up a smoke out of his nostrils, and fire out of his mouth devoured: coals were kindled by it. He bowed the heavens also, and came down; and darkness was under his feet" (2 Sam. 22:6-10).

Chapter 8
Out of Hell

At that very moment, it was almost like hell itself vomited me out. Incredibly it felt like I was being shot out of a canon. The next thing I knew, I was standing on the edge of a high and steep cliff. No longer was I in hell, but I was standing on the lip of a cliff looking straight down into the ocean of torment I had just been suffering in. The ocean of hell was still bubbling, boiling, and churning. And I could feel some of the heat of it hitting my body. The stench of it was still suffocating. I would say that the cliff was probably over a thousand feet high. As a looked around, I noticed that the land around me was virtually flat, with no vegetation. It all looked like it was compacted brownish, gray soil, with rocks and boulders. As I looked behind me there seemed to be a mountain range on the far horizon. As I looked to my right side, I noticed that in the distance there was what looked to be a wide, dark, slow-flowing river. It was pouring its contents like Niagara Falls over the edge of the cliff into the yawning mouth of hell.

But there was something very strange and eerie about this river. I did not want anything to do with this river. Actually there was this overwhelming desire in my heart to run as far away from it as I could. I knew that there was something very wrong about what I was seeing. In my heart I sensed that whatever the river was, it would bring to me tremendous pain and sorrow perhaps even more so than what I had experienced in the bottomless pit of hell. And yet, with this knowledge, this foreboding and dread in my heart, I knew that I must go to this river. The Spirit of God was prompting me to go and investigate. So instead of running away from this river, I found myself walking along the edge of the cliff, toward the river. As I got closer and closer, I began to tremble and shake. I could barely breathe. I had to take short gasps of breath. I could not believe, and I did not want to believe what I was seeing before my very eyes.

Broad and Wide Road

This broad and wide, dark river was not flowing with water, as I had supposed. It was made up of multitudes and multitudes of people. Masses of humanity without number.

> *"Enter ye in at the strait gate: for wide is the gate, and broad is the way, that leadeth to destruction, and many there be which go in thereat" (Matt. 7:13).*

I could see that there were those of all nations, tongues and peoples. I saw the dress of every religious group you could imagine. Upon this road there was a range of people who were both young and elderly. And by looking at their mannerisms and dress, you could determine to some extent what their livelihoods were. There were people of all professions—doctors, nurses, plumbers, professors, pastors, teachers, housewives, factory workers, policemen, farmers, milk men, bankers, military personnel, politicians, and world rulers.

> *"And he saith unto me, The waters which thou sawest, where the whore sitteth, are peoples,*

*and multitudes, and nations, and tongues"
(Rev. 17:15).*

*"Multitudes, multitudes in the valley of decision:
for the day of the LORD is near in the valley of
decision" (Joel 3:14).*

Praise God I did not see any infants, little children in
the masses of people. Christ said that in heaven there is no
giving in marriage.

*"Jesus answered and said unto them, Ye do
err, not knowing the scriptures, nor the power
of God. For in the resurrection they neither
marry, nor are given in marriage, but are as
the angels of God in heaven"
(Matt. 22:29-30).*

And yet the Scriptures refer to little ones being
in the new heaven and in the new earth. In my study
and research of the Scriptures when a little child or
an infant dies before the age of accountability (what
ever that age may be), they automatically ascend to
heaven. Our little girl, Naomi, went home to be with
the Lord when she was four and a half years old in the
year 2000. I can hardly wait to hold her once again in
my arms. I personally believe when a little one dies,
they remain as children throughout eternity. Those
who were aborted or had miscarriages might be two
to four years old.

The question may arise, *what happened to their
sinful nature?* You see the sinful nature was in their flesh.
And they left the Earth before they knowingly and willingly
yielded to the demonic seed of sin. Therefore it did not
follow them into eternity.

89

*"The wolf also shall dwell with the lamb, and
the leopard shall lie down with the kid; and the
calf and the young lion and the fatling together;
and a little child shall lead them. And the cow
and the bear shall feed; their young ones shall
lie down together: and the lion shall eat straw
like the ox. And the sucking child shall play on
the hole of the asp, and the weaned child shall
put his hand on the cockatrice' den. They shall
not hurt nor destroy in all my holy mountain:
for the earth shall be full of the knowledge of
the Lord, as the waters cover the sea"*
(Isa. 11:6-9).

I believe we will discover this amazing truth when we get
there. I do not believe that this is just a happy thought. The
Scripture declares that Christ lights every soul of every man
that comes into this world. Every soul is born alive onto God.
And when a person willingly and knowingly rebels against
God, according to the Scriptures, that soul dies. If there is a
scriptural basis to believe otherwise, I'm more than willing to
accept it. This is just something that I have a strong feeling
about. I believe we can wholeheartedly encourage those who
have lost little ones with these truths.

*"That was the true Light, which lighteth every
man that cometh into the world" (John 1:9).*

As I drew nearer and nearer to this river, I could see
that the people were walking on what looked to be a very
wide asphalt road that made its winding way as far as my
eyes could see into the horizon. Every inch of the road was
packed to capacity with humanity, like sardines in a can. It
seemed almost impossible for people to be packed so tight
and so close together.

Now this road came right to the very edge of the cliff. At the cliff it broke off with jagged edges hanging over emptiness. It looked like a road would if an earthquake had transpired with the earth dropping out from underneath a major highway! And below this broken highway was the yawning, never-satisfied mouth of hell.

Headed to Destruction

As I came closer to this river of humanity I found myself unconsciously looking deep into the faces of those who were walking on this broad and wide road. None of them, I literally mean that none of them seemed to be in the least bit concerned at all about where they were headed. They did not seem to be concerned about their future or where they were going. They did not seem to question the direction in which they were walking. Many were laughing and jesting. Others simply engrossed in conversation. Others caught up in their own problems. As I looked upon their faces I could perceive in my heart who they were and what they were going through. I knew in my heart that by the Spirit of God I was experiencing their sorrows, pains, loneliness, and depression. I also perceived the hopes, dreams, and visions that they had in their hearts, that which they had not yet apprehended or achieved. But not one of them seemed to be concerned about what was about to happen. Or where they were going. It was as if they were sleepwalking, like they were slumbering not realizing the danger that was just before them. It was as if they were blind to their eternal damnation.

"And the cares of this world, and the deceitfulness of riches, and the lusts of other things entering in, choke the word, and it becometh unfruitful" (Mark 4:19).

"And he spake a parable unto them, saying, The ground of a certain rich man brought forth plentifully: And he thought within himself, saying, What shall I do, because I have no room where to bestow my fruits? And he said, This will I do: I will pull down my barns, and build greater; and there will I bestow all my fruits and my goods. And I will say to my soul, Soul, thou hast much goods laid up for many years; take thine ease, eat, drink, and be merry. But God said unto him, Thou fool, this night thy soul shall be required of thee: then whose shall those things be, which thou hast provided? So is he that layeth up treasure for himself, and is not rich toward God" (Luke 12:16-21).

At about twenty feet from the end of the road a small handful of them would seem to begin to wake up. At that moment it would become a totally different story. The reality of the situation seemed to finally dawn upon their faces. As they were pushed forward they began to try to push back against the oncoming masses. And the more they were pushed forward, the more frantic they became. They began to scream and cry and yell for help. But it was too late; they could not detach themselves from the masses. They were pushed forward, inch by inch, foot by foot. Those on the very edge of the cliff would seem to lose their mind in absolute terror as they saw more clearly what was awaiting them at the bottom of the cliff. It was as if their eyes were popping out of their head.

Never have I seen faces so contorted with absolute horror and fear. I knew they could not believe what they were seeing. They began to push back with all of their might, clawing, hitting, scratching, trying to crawl over the top of those who were unwillingly pushing them to their destruction and damnation. Screams of unbelievable horror came from their lips as they would try to hang on. Shouting and screaming with such deep desperation that it breaks my heart retelling it to you. It did not seem as if those who were only a few feet back could hear or see what was taking place until it was their turn. Or maybe they simply chose to ignore the commotion, because it did not yet involve them. They were so caught up in their daily living until destruction came upon them without warning.

"For when they shall say, Peace and safety; then sudden destruction cometh upon them, as travail upon a woman with child; and they shall not escape" (1 Thess. 5:3).

"But as the days of Noah were, so shall also the coming of the Son of man be. For as in the days that were before the flood they were eating and drinking, marrying and giving in marriage, until the day that Noah entered into the ark, And knew not until the flood came, and took them all away; so shall also the coming of the Son of man be" (Matt. 24:37-39).

A number of years ago I came across an older book about the testimonies of saints and sinners dying on their deathbeds. In that time period in which this book was written the medical world did not yet have medication to sedate people in their last painful moments. This book was both glorious and excruciatingly painful. It gave wonderful accounts of saints crying out with joy and excitement as they saw angels coming for them. Sometimes they would see Jesus. And at other times it would be a loved one or ones who had already gone home to be with the Lord.

These loved ones would meet them at their deathbeds to accompany them to heaven.

Yet there were those who were not right with God. They would scream with absolute and utter terror as demons came for them. Many of them would begin to scream as they began to experience the flames and agonies of hell before they took their last breath.

Into the Abyss

As the people on the broad and wide asphalt road fell over the jagged edge, I watched them dig their fingernails into its unyielding surface. Not being able to hold on, they would continue to claw at the rough cliff walls. Leaving trails of their precious human blood. The cliff wall was covered and matted with human blood, flesh, and bones. You could hear their pitiful screams for help as they tried to stop their descent into hell. As they plunged toward hell I would watch them spinning and tumbling head over heels. No horror flick ever made could express the absolute terror and horror I was watching take place before my eyes. These peoples' worst nightmares were coming to pass— nightmares that would last throughout eternity.

When their bodies hit the burning, liquefied lava of hell it would create a splash like that of a rock dropping into a puddle of mud. For a few seconds I could see them struggling, still floating on the surface of the lake of lava, like a leaf on the water. Their clothes would catch on fire. Their hair would go up in flames and be consumed. Their identities were lost. No longer could you tell that they were male or female. Their nationalities, their ages, even the color of their skin was devoured in the burning torments of hell. Oh you cannot believe the terrible, heart-wrenching screams as they hit the surface and began to burn. They would slowly sink into the burning mud of hell, swallowed up in the never-ending undercurrents of this ocean of damnation. These were men and women, young and old, grandmas and grandpas, and teenagers. These were people of all nations and cultures from every diverse aspect of life. For hell is not a respecter of people.

Hell Enlarging

If this in itself is not horrible enough, then even more heart wrenching is the fact that this river of humanity is seemingly never-ending. Neither does it slow up. It just keeps flowing unrelentingly, as far as the eye could see. At the time if I had a pair of binoculars, I still would not have been able to see the end to this road. I have read somewhere that there is an estimated 6.6 billion people on the Earth right now.[15] Out of that number, over 235,000 people are dying every day.[16] If it takes you five hours to read this book, by the time you finish reading, over 48,955 people will have died and gone to their eternal destiny. That means 9,791 people die every hour, and 163 people die every minute. Out of 6.6 billion people only 350 million confess to be Protestant Christians. How many of them truly love God and have forsaken the world? Only God truly knows.

Many years ago I met a gentleman by the name of Howard Pittman. He spoke in our church and shared with us this testimony. On August 3, 1979, Howard had a death experience. While the physicians were trying to save his life because of a terrible accident, he died! In this state of death, he was permitted to watch fifty saints (true Christians) enter into heaven. It was explained to him that "at the same time those fifty saints died on Earth, 1,950 other humans also died; or only fifty out of two thousand made it into heaven. The other 1,950 were not there."[17]

Based on his experience in 1979 at that time, only about one in forty were making it to heaven. Fifty of two thousand is about 2.5% saints, true Christians, going to heaven. That means 97.5% were going somewhere else.

> *"Because strait is the gate, and narrow is the way, which leadeth unto life, and few there be that find it" (Matt. 7:14).*

So many are going to hell that Scripture implies hell has to enlarge itself to accommodate all those who are descending into its misery. I believe that is why there has been an increase in earthquakes and volcanic activity. Hell is growing to such an extent to where Earth itself is going through tremendous upheavals. There will be more and more earthquakes and volcanoes erupting as we watch the masses of humanity die. Lately there have been earth-shattering earthquakes around the world. These will trigger even more quakes because the death of those taking place in these earthquakes cause hell to expand even more.

> *"Therefore hell hath enlarged herself, and opened her mouth without measure: and their glory, and their multitude, and their pomp, and he that rejoiceth, shall descend into it"*
> *(Isa. 5:14).*

> *"Hell and destruction are never full"*
> *(Prov. 27:20a).*

Chapter 9
God's Heart Broken

As I watched these masses of humanity falling into the bottomless pit of hell I literally could not handle it. I ran from the edge of the cliff alongside this road of damned humanity like one who has lost his mind. I wanted to escape the sight of the pain and agony etched in peoples' faces as they were falling over the cliff. My heart felt like it was totally and mortally wounded. I felt like I was being stabbed with a huge knife that was slowly twisting and turning inside of me in my heart. My heart felt like it was being torn out of my chest. Now, if I felt this way, can you imagine how God feels? People believe that after Jesus suffered on the cross that He no longer suffers. But this is a sadly mistaken assumption. For the Father, Son, and the Holy Ghost are still in deep agony and pain over the fate of humanity. God's heart is broken over the loss of humanity and of the angelic realm that disobeyed and rebelled against Him.

"In all their affliction he was afflicted"
(Isa. 63:9a).

"For we have not an high priest which cannot be touched with the feeling of our infirmities; but was in all points tempted like as we are, yet without sin" (Heb. 4:15).

But if God knew that this was going to be the end result, why would He create the angelic realm and humanity? For me to share with you the ultimate purpose and conclusion of God's plan would take a book within itself. I'll do the best I can with a quick explanation. Because God Himself is the giver, He wants to share all that He has with His creation. The only problem is that His creation cannot handle all that He has.

Lucifer is a major example. The little bit of glory, position, and power that God gave to this archangel ultimately became his downfall. Of course, Lucifer and the angels that followed him have no excuse. They knew in their hearts what they were doing was evil and wrong. That is why they are not given an opportunity for salvation. The moment they rebelled against God and sinned against heaven, they were eternally locked into their damnable natures. It would be like taking pure water and dumping black ink into it. You can never make it clear and clean again.

God wants to share His wealth, abundance, power, and glory that He was willing to pay the ultimate price to bring about a creation that would love Him. They would love Him to such an extent that no matter how He blessed them, they would not rise up against Him. He could cause them to become one with Him and yet be totally submitted in every area of their existence. It would have to be a creation that had already been tempted, tested, and tried. It would contain those who had experienced the evil of selfishness and rejected it in order to love their Creator. Beloved, this is what it's all about. We choose to love God more than ourselves or the pleasures of this present time. Therefore we are esteemed worthy of all that God is, has, or ever will be. According to the Scriptures we will rule and reign with Christ forever. Simply because He first loved us. We rise up against the sinful nature that is in our flesh, which has penetrated our souls, following our beloved Savior and Shepherd wherever He may lead.

Sufferings of Christ

The suffering of Christ is still a great mystery to many of those in the church even. This suffering did not begin in the garden of Gethsemane. It literally began before the creation of all things. The Scriptures declared He was slain before the foundations of the world.

> *"And all that dwell upon the earth shall worship him, whose names are not written in the book of life of the Lamb slain from the foundation of the world" (Rev 13:8).*

> *"But with the precious blood of Christ, as of a lamb without blemish and without spot: Who verily was foreordained before the foundation of the world, but was manifest in these last times for you" (1 Pet. 1:19-20).*

From His birth to His resurrection Jesus Christ has suffered for you and me. In Isaiah chapter 53 it says He was a man of sorrows and acquainted with grief. It broke His heart to see the masses of humanity reject Him as their Messiah. For He knew that there was no other way than through Himself for men to be saved. We can only become partakers of the divine nature through the seed of Christ within the soil of our hearts.

It truly is all about Jesus. I would challenge every believer to buy a new Bible, and with a yellow highlighter, highlight every time it refers to Jesus in an intimate and personal way beginning in Matthew through the end of the book of Revelation. You would be amazed and shocked to discover that the Scriptures refer to Jesus approximately ten thousand times. That's ten thousand times in approximately 350 pages.

As we see Jesus moving toward His ultimate sacrifice, His personal suffering increased. The night He was betrayed by Judas, He sweat great drops of blood (see Luke 24:44). He declared that His soul was close to death because of His suffering. All of the sins of humanity were being poured into Him. He never committed sin, but Scripture says that He was made sin that we might be made to be partakers of His righteousness. All of His suffering—the stripes upon His back, the crown of thorns upon His head, His beard being ripped out of His face, the spitting mocking and bruising of His body, dragging that rugged cross up Golgotha's hill— was for our salvation. When they threw His body down upon the tree and nailed His feet and hands to it with spikes, Christ, God in the flesh, allowed Himself to be brutalized and violated for our salvation. Even the heavenly Father had to turn His back upon His own son. Can you imagine how it broke the Father's heart for Him to have to turn His back on His only begotten Son?

> *"And about the ninth hour Jesus cried with a loud voice, saying, Eli, Eli, lama sabachthani? that is to say, My God, my God, why hast thou forsaken me?" (Matt. 27:46).*

How could any human being not love Him? But that was not the end of His suffering. Scripture declares His soul descended into hell. This is very important for us to understand. His Spirit did not descend into hell, but it returned to the Father from which it came.

> *"And when Jesus had cried with a loud voice, he said, Father, into thy hands I commend my*

spirit: and having said thus, he gave up the spirit" (Luke 23:46).

"He seeing this before spake of the resurrection of Christ, that his soul was not left in hell, neither his flesh did see corruption. This Jesus hath God raised up, whereof we all are witnesses" (Acts 2:31-32).

The reason why there is so much confusion in some of these areas of understanding is because we have not rightly discerned the Word of truth. Many years ago I discovered not to wrestle with the Word but simply to acknowledge, and believe, even if it contradicts everything I've ever been taught. I simply embrace the truth no matter where it leads. And then God gives me understanding within the context of those Scriptures. It is a wonderful and beautiful freedom. It is only when we allow the philosophy and indoctrination of naturally thinking men, which contradicts the teaching of God's Word, to influence our lives that we wrestle with the scriptures. This also gives the enemy of our soul, the devil, the right to blind our eyes from the truth.

The soul of Christ took the sins of humanity into the depths of hell to be left there forever. Jesus is able to help us because He knows the pains and sufferings of not only life but separation from the Father. He knows the torments of hell. Surely we can trust our eternal souls to such a loving Savior.

Tri-unity of Man

The Scriptures reveal that man is a three-part being. The three parts of man are composed of his soul, spirit, and body. There seems to be a lot of misunderstanding over man's three-part composition. Virtually, a book alone could be written on this particular subject. For us to truly comprehend what hell is all about we need to understand who and what man is. Really the Scriptures are quite informative and descriptive pertaining to this area. (Many times our indoctrination interferes with this revelation.)

When my wife and I attended Bible college, we were taught that we were a spirit, that we have a soul, and that we live in a physical body. If you diligently search the Scriptures I think you will discover that this is not the correct makeup of man's composition.

Man is a soul.

Over eleven hundred times within the Scriptures the Bible talks about man's soul. We only need to use a small portion of the Scriptures to reveal the truth about this divine mystery. Genesis declared that man became a living soul. The soul of man is also considered his heart—our thoughts, intents, and purposes, that which decides and determines our eternal destiny.

> *"And the LORD God formed man of the dust of the ground, and breathed into his nostrils the breath of life; and man became a living soul"* *(Gen. 2:7).*

> *"And so it is written, The first man Adam was made a living soul; the last Adam was made a quickening spirit" (1 Cor. 15:45).*

It is the soul of man that commits sin. It is also the soul of man that dies. The Spirit of the Lord in man did not die as many have been taught. When man committed sin in the garden, he was warned that he would die. It was the soul that God was warning him about. At

102

that moment the human soul died to its responsiveness, sensitivity, and love for God. The heart and soul received the corruptible seed of Satan and became a lover of self and the flesh. The controlling and dominating aspect of the human soul came under the influence of corrupted flesh, where at one time it was under the influence of God's Spirit.

"The soul that sinneth, it shall die"
(Ezek. 18:20a).

"And you hath he quickened, who were dead in trespasses and sins; Wherein in time past ye walked according to the course of this world, according to the prince of the power of the air, the spirit that now worketh in the children of disobedience: Among whom also we all had our conversation in times past in the lusts of our flesh, fulfilling the desires of the flesh and of the mind; and were by nature the children of wrath, even as others" (Eph. 2:1-3).

It is the soul of man that goes to hell and not the spirit. The unconverted souls of humanity are eternally separated from God and quarantined in hell.

It is the soul (the heart) of man that must be converted. It is in the soul that believers experience a new birth. The incorruptible seed of God's divine nature must be implanted into the soil of the soul of man. Our souls must be converted, transformed, renewed, and saved. Jesus came to save our souls.

"Brethren, if any of you do err from the truth, and one convert him; Let him know, that he which converteth the sinner from the error of

103

his way shall save a soul from death, and shall hide a multitude of sins" (James 5:19-20).

"Receiving the end of your faith, even the salvation of your souls" (1 Pet. 1:9).

Please keep in mind that when the Scriptures are talking about the human soul it is referring to the human heart.

"The heart is deceitful above all things, and desperately wicked: who can know it?"
(Jer. 17:9).

"This is an evil among all things that are done under the sun, that there is one event unto all: yea, also the heart of the sons of men is full of evil, and madness is in their heart while they live, and after that they go to the dead"
(Eccles. 9:3).

The human soul is one of God's most amazing creations. It bridges the gap of the spiritual and the natural. It literally straddles both dimensions. The human soul was created to house the very essence of God Himself. The Scriptures declare that we are His tabernacle. We are to be the dwelling place of God's presence. The demonic world wanted to sit upon God's throne. That's why they endeavor to possess our souls. In order to get a glimpse of the capacity of the human soul we just need to take a look at the example within the Scriptures. When Jesus cast the devils out of the man from the region of the Gadarenes, the demons declared that they were a legion. In that particular time a full strength of a legion of Roman soldiers was officially made up of 5,200 men. [18]

Could it possibly be that this man's soul was inhabited by six thousand devils? Yes, I believe he was. This reveals the capacity of the human soul, which was made to be inhabited by God's Spirit.

Man has a spirit.

The word *spirit* is used many times within the Bible. You have to study the context to see what it is referring to. It could be referring to angelic, demonic, the Holy Spirit, or the human spirit. It can also be referring to the attitude or the disposition of a person. A perfect example is when Scripture says that Joshua and Caleb had a different spirit about them.

"But my servant Caleb, because he had another spirit with him, and hath followed me fully, him will I bring into the land whereinto he went; and his seed shall possess it" (Num. 14:24).

"We having the same spirit of faith, according as it is written, I believed, and therefore have I spoken; we also believe, and therefore speak" (2 Cor. 4:13).

In the Garden of Eden, God breathed into man the breath of life. When the soul of man died in the garden, he did not lose the Spirit of God. The Spirit of God still resides in his flesh. Actually the Spirit of God is the life of the flesh. It is only when the Spirit leaves man that the flesh will die. The human spirit is similar to electricity in the sense that it provides the active energy of the human flesh. Of course it is much deeper than this simple statement.

"The burden of the word of the LORD for Israel, saith the LORD, which stretcheth forth the heavens, and layeth the foundation of the earth, and formeth the spirit of man within him" (Zech. 12:1).

"The Spirit of God hath made me, and the breath of the Almighty hath given me life" (Job 33:4).

The spirit within man is the conscience of his heart. It is to be the divine guidance system for his soul given by God. It is the "GPS of man's life." The spirit that God put within man's flesh never died. Men throughout the ages have either yielded or ignored the voice of His Spirit. As I stated there needs to be a whole book written on this particular subject. The description that I am giving here is really an oversimplification of the deep mysteries of the kingdom of God. Man is fearfully and wonderfully made.

"But there is a spirit in man: and the inspiration of the Almighty giveth them understanding" (Job 32:8).

"For what man knoweth the things of a man, save the spirit of man which is in him? even so the things of God knoweth no man, but the Spirit of God" (1 Cor. 2:11).

When a person dies outside of Christ the spirit returns to God from whence it came. But his soul goes to hell. The soul (heart) is who you really are. The human spirit is not re-created at the new birth. The spirit of man never died; it was his soul. Our souls need to be born again. Our souls need to be saved.

106

"Then shall the dust return to the earth as it was: and the spirit shall return unto God who gave it" (Eccles. 12:7).

"If he set his heart upon man, if he gather unto himself his spirit and his breath; All flesh shall perish together, and man shall turn again unto dust" (Job 34:14-15). [This is referring to his body!]

Man inhabits a body.

Yes, the human body is an amazing machine. But the simple truth is that it was not created through a process of evolution. It was created by the spirit that God breathed into it. And when you and I die, the human body will turn back to dust from whence it came. Then at the return of Christ those who are saved will receive a glorified body. But those who are damned will not receive an indestructible body till after the thousand-year reign of Christ. Then their souls with their re-created bodies will be cast into the lake of fire with the devil and his angels for all eternity.

"Thou hidest thy face, they are troubled: thou takest away their breath, they die, and return to their dust" (Ps. 104:29).

"And many of them that sleep in the dust of the earth shall awake, some to everlasting life, and some to shame and everlasting contempt" (Dan. 12: 2).

The conclusion of what we have just briefly studied is that you and I are a soul. We have a spirit that comes from God Almighty. And we are housed in a physical body.

Christ died to save our souls. When a person dies loving Christ, his soul becomes one with the Spirit of God for eternity. It is like that of the seed of man, entering into the egg of the woman, thereby creating a human life. The new birth and the life of the believer is similar in that a son of God comes forth. We enter into an immortal eternal life. And our corrupted body will put on incorruption, and mortality will put on immortality.

Chapter 10
I Have to Do Something

I ran from the dreadful scene before my eyes. I ran until I could run no more. Out of breath I finally slowed to a walk. As I continued to walk, I realized that I must do something about these masses and masses of people that were headed straight to hell. I was still walking alongside this wide, broad, river of humanity but away from the cliff. So I began to shout to them, pleading and begging them to come off the road. I warned the people with all the compassion of my heart, with tears cascading down my face, flowing like a river, weeping, and pleading nonstop.

"Oh that my head were waters, and mine eyes a fountain of tears, that I might weep day and night for the slain of the daughter of my people!" (Jer. 9:1).

"Rivers of waters run down mine eyes, because they keep not thy law" (Ps. 119:136).

I tried everything I could, knowing that every minute that passed more and more people were falling over the cliff. And because I had experienced the pains and torments of hell I knew what they were about to experience and that they would never get out. I was preaching the thunder and the lightning of heaven. Then I would speak the love and mercy of the goodness of God. I preached the reality of Jesus and His atoning sacrificial work. With all the truths that I had available I declared God's kingdom that I might rescue some.

Would Not Listen

Many of these people on the road would stare at me as if I had lost my mind. Some would yell back at me, telling me to mind my own business. Some yelled that they were Christians, and that they were going to heaven. And others would seem to listen, with tears flowing down their cheeks. They would say that they wanted to come off of the broad and wide way, but they could not, that their hearts were too addicted to sin. They did not believe that Jesus had the power to deliver them, that they were beyond hope. Some said that they had blasphemed the Holy Ghost and therefore there was no salvation available for them. Others declared that they loved sin too much to let go of it. The demonic hordes were whispering in their ears, lying to them that God would not forgive them, that they were too far gone, or that hell was just a make-believe imaginary place.

> *"But if our gospel be hid, it is hid to them that are lost: In whom the god of this world hath blinded the minds of them which believe not, lest the light of the glorious gospel of Christ, who is the image of God, should shine unto them"* (2 Cor. 4:3-4).

Laborers Few

I knew in my heart that the work before me was too great for one person alone. I desperately needed help to reach these this multitude of lost souls. One person by

110

himself could not make barely a dent in evangelizing this ocean of humanity. I began searching to find someone, anyone, who could help me reach all these people.

I later came across this excerpt about William Booth who God used to start the Salvation Army. He had an amazing vision similar to mine.

On one of my recent journeys, as I gazed from the coach window, I was led into a train of thought concerning the condition of the multitudes around me. They were living carelessly in the most open and shameless rebellion against God, without a thought for their eternal welfare.

As I looked out of the window, I seemed to see them all...millions of people all around me given up to their drink and their pleasure, their dancing and their music, their business and their anxieties, their politics and their troubles. Ignorant- willfully ignorant in many cases- and in other instances knowing all about the truth and not caring at all. But all of them, the whole mass of them, sweeping on and up in their blasphemies and devilries to the Throne of God. While my mind was thus engaged, I had a vision.

I saw a dark and stormy ocean. Over it the black clouds hung heavily; through them every now and then vivid lightening flashed and loud thunder rolled, while the winds moaned, and the waves rose and foamed, towered and broke, only to rise and foam, tower and break again.

In that ocean I thought I saw myriads of poor human beings plunging and floating, shouting and shrieking, cursing and struggling and drowning; and as they cursed and screamed they rose and shrieked again, and then some sank to rise no more.

And I saw out of this dark angry ocean, a mighty rock that rose up with its summit towering high above the black clouds that overhung the stormy sea. And all around the base of this great rock I saw a vast platform. Onto this platform, I saw with delight a number of the poor struggling, drowning wretches continually climbing out of the angry ocean. And I saw that a few of those who were already safe on the platform were helping the poor creatures still in the angry waters to reach the place of safety.

On looking more closely I found a number of those who had been rescued, industriously working and scheming by ladders, ropes, boats and other means more effective, to deliver the poor strugglers out of the sea. Here and there were some who actually jumped into the water, regardless of the consequences in their passion to "rescue the perishing." And I hardly know which gladdened me the most- the sight of the poor drowning people climbing onto the rocks reaching a place of safety, or the devotion and self-sacrifice of those whose whole being was wrapped up in the effort for their deliverance.

As I looked on, I saw that the occupants of that platform were quite a mixed company. That is, they were divided into different "sets" or classes, and they occupied themselves with different pleasures and employments. But only a very few of them seemed to make it their business to get the people out of the sea.

But what puzzled me most was the fact that though all of them had been rescued at one time or another from the ocean, nearly everyone seemed to have forgotten all about it. Anyway, it seemed the memory of its darkness and danger no longer troubled them at all. And what seemed equally strange and perplexing to me was that these people did not even seem to have any care- that is any agonizing care- about the poor perishing ones who were struggling and drowning right before their very eyes...many of whom were their own husbands and wives, brothers and sisters and even their own children.

Now this astonishing unconcern could not have been the result of ignorance or lack of knowledge, because they lived right there in full sight of it all and even talked about it sometimes. Many even went regularly to hear lectures and sermons in which the awful state of these poor drowning creatures was described.

I have always said that the occupants of this platform were engaged in different pursuits and pastimes. Some of them were absorbed day and night in trading and business in order to make gain, storing up their savings in boxes, safes and the like.

Many spent their time in amusing themselves with growing flowers on the side of the rock, others in painting pieces of cloth or in playing music, or in dressing themselves up in different styles and walking about to be admired. Some occupied themselves chiefly in eating and drinking, others were taken up with arguing about the poor drowning creatures that had already been rescued.

But the thing to me that seemed the most amazing was that those on the platform to whom He called, who heard His voice and felt that they ought to obey it- at least they said they did- those who confessed to love Him much were in full sympathy with Him in the task He had undertaken- who worshipped Him or who professed to do so- were so taken up with their trades and professions, their money saving and pleasures, their families and circles, their religions and arguments about it, and their preparation for going to the mainland, that they did not listen to the cry that came to them from this Wonderful Being who had Himself gone down into the sea. Anyway, if they heard it they did not heed it. They did not care. And so the multitude went on right before them struggling and shrieking and drowning in the darkness.

And then I saw something that seemed to me even more strange than anything that had gone on before in this strange vision. I saw that some of these people on the platform whom this Wonderful Being had called to, wanting them to come and help Him in His difficult task of saving these perishing creatures, were always praying and crying out to Him to come to them!
Some wanted Him to come and stay with them, and spend His time and strength in making them happier. Others wanted Him to come and take away various doubts and misgivings they had concerning the truth of some letters He had written them. Some wanted Him to come and make them feel more secure on the rock- so secure that they would be quite sure that they should never slip off again into the ocean. Numbers of others wanted Him to make them feel quite certain that they would really get off the rock and onto the mainland

someday: because as a matter of fact, it was well known that some had walked so carelessly as to loose their footing, and had fallen back again into the stormy waters.

So these people used to meet and get up as high on the rock as they could, and looking towards the mainland (where they thought the Great Being was) they would cry out, "Come to us! Come and help us!" And all the while He was down (by His Spirit) among the poor struggling, drowning creatures in the angry deep, with His arms around them trying to drag them out, and looking up- oh! so longingly but all in vain- to those on the rock, crying to them with His voice all hoarse from calling, "Come to Me! Come, and help Me!"

And then I understood it all. It was plain enough. The sea was the ocean of life- the sea of real, actual human existence. That lightening was the gleaming of piercing truth coming from Jehovah's Throne. That thunder was the distant echoing of the wrath of God. Those multitudes of people shrieking, struggling and agonizing in the stormy sea, was the thousands and thousands of poor harlots and harlot-makers, of drunkards and drunkard makers, of thieves, liars, blasphemers and ungodly people of every kindred, tongue and nation.

Oh what a black sea it was! And oh, what multitudes of rich and poor, ignorant and educated were there. They were all so unalike in their outward circumstances and conditions, yet all alike in one thing- all sinners before God- all held by, and holding onto, some iniquity, fascinated by some idol, the slaves of some devilish lust, and ruled by the foul fiend from the bottomless pit!

"All alike in one thing?" No, all alike in two things- not only the same in their wickedness but, unless rescued, the same in their sinking, sinking... down, down, down... to the same terrible doom. That great sheltering rock represented Calvary, the place where Jesus had died for them. And the people on it were those who had been rescued. The way they used their energies, gifts and time represented the occupations and amusements of those who professed to be saved from sin and hell- followers of the Lord Jesus Christ. The handful of fierce, determined ones, who were risking their own lives in saving the perishing were true soldiers of the cross of Jesus. That Mighty Being who was calling to them from the midst of the angry waters was the Son of God, "the same yesterday, today and forever" who is still struggling and interceding to save the dying multitudes about us from this terrible doom of damnation, and whose voice can be heard above the music, machinery, and noise of life, calling on the rescued to come and help Him save the world.

My friends in Christ, you are rescued from the waters, you are on the rock, He is in the dark sea calling on you to come to Him and help Him. Will you go? Look for yourselves. The surging sea of life, crowded with perishing multitudes rolls up to the very spot on which you stand. Leaving the vision, I now come to speak of the fact- a fact that is as real as the Bible, as real as the Christ who hung upon the cross, as real as the judgment day will be, and as real as the heaven and hell that will follow it.

Look! Don't be deceived by appearances- men and things are not what they seem. All who are not on the rock are in the sea! Look at them from the standpoint of the great White Throne, and what a sight you have! Jesus Christ, the Son of God is, through His Spirit, in the midst of this dying multitude, struggling to save them. And He is calling on you to jump into the sea- to go right away to His side and help Him in the holy strife. Will you jump? That is, will you go to His feet and place yourself absolutely at His disposal?

A young Christian once came to me, and told me that for some time she had been giving the Lord her profession and prayers and money, but now she wanted to give Him her life. She wanted to go right into the fight. In other words, she wanted to go to His assistance in the sea. As when a man from the shore, seeing another struggling in the water, takes off those outer garments that would hinder his efforts and leaps to the rescue, so will you who still linger on the bank, thinking and singing and praying about the poor perishing souls, lay aside your shame, your pride, your cares about other people's opinions, your love of ease and all the selfish loves that have kept you back for so long, and rush to the rescue of this multitude of dying men and women.

Does the surging sea look dark and dangerous? Unquestionably it is so. There is no *doubt that the leap for you, as for everyone who takes it, means difficulty and scorn and suffering. For you it may mean more than this. It may mean death. He who beckons you from the sea however, knows what it will mean - and knowing, He still calls to you and bids to you to come.*

You must do it! You cannot hold back. You have enjoyed yourself in Christianity long enough. You have had pleasant feelings, pleasant songs, pleasant meetings, pleasant prospects. There has been much of human happiness, much clapping of hands and shouting of praises- very much of heaven on earth.

Now then, go to God and tell Him you are prepared as much as necessary to turn your back upon it all, and that you are willing to spend the rest of your days struggling in the midst of these perishing multitudes, whatever it may cost you.

You must do it. With the light that is now broken in upon your mind and the call that is now sounding in your ears, and the beckoning hands that are now before your eyes, you have no alternative. To go down among the perishing crowds is your duty. Your happiness from now on will consist in sharing their misery, your ease in sharing their pain, your crown in helping them to bear their cross, and your heaven in going into the very jaws of hell to rescue them. Now, I ask you, what will you do? [19]

Clusters of Saints

As I looked out across the flat plateaus, I could see clusters of objects in the distance. I could not make out what they were, but they seemed to be shining with a brilliant white. They were not on the broad and wide road but directly off to the side of it. As I moved farther up the road I saw that these white objects were in what appeared to be small and large groupings. And as I looked out over the plain, I noticed there were more of these clusters. Not just one or two but hundreds of them were scattered across the horizon. Some appeared to be extremely large, others were very small with many different sizes in between. As I drew closer to the first one, I discerned there was some type of movement taking place in these brilliant white clusters. As I drew closer it became apparent to me what they were.

These clusters were made up of people wearing glistening white robes. They were all grouped together in circles, facing inward, sometimes back to back. Their backs were to the river of humanity walking on the broad and wide road and to all else. The closer I came near these clusters, the more it became clear what was happening. Many of those within these clusters had their hands lifted up toward heaven. As I got closer I could see smiles of joy radiating from their faces. Tears were running down their cheeks. They were singing amazing and beautiful songs of love for Christ. At times one or more would break out in what seemed to be a prophetic Word.

From what I could hear, most of these songs were about how much God loved them and about the blessings that would overtake them in their walk with the Lord. These songs said that they were precious and important to Jesus and to the heavenly Father. I realized automatically who these people in white must be. They were fellow believers and saints in Christ—brothers and sisters in Jesus Christ. All of these clusters of saints seemed to be lost in their devotion to and for God.

But they seemed to be lost, totally and completely oblivious to the masses of humanity that were just a few feet away from them being led to an everlasting, never-ending, eternal damnation. They were enraptured in their own little spiritual experiences. They were enthralled with singing songs of praise and worship. There was no denying the sincerity; it was evident in their involvement and enthusiasm. But what good is sincerity, blessings, joyful spiritual experiences, and Holy Ghost parties if you are not concerned about anyone else except your own little group. It's what Scripture refers to as sounding brass and twinkling cymbals.

"Though I speak with the tongues of men and of angels, and have not charity, I am become as sounding brass, or a tinkling cymbal. And though I have the gift of prophecy, and understand all mysteries, and all knowledge; and though I have all faith, so that I could remove mountains, and have not charity, I am nothing. And though I bestow all my goods to feed the poor, and though I give my body to be burned, and have not charity, it profiteth me nothing" (1 Cor. 13:1-3).

A divine and supernatural urgency rose up in my heart. I tried to push my way into one of these clusters. And as I did I found myself yelling and pointing to the river of humanity. It was not anger, self-righteousness, or disgust that moved me but God's love. It was His overwhelming love and compassion that was being shed abroad in my heart by the Holy Ghost. It was love for the unconverted, lost, and blind sinners.

I desperately needed help to reach the lost masses upon the road of destruction. I knew in my heart that the heart of God was being broken because His people were not having compassion upon those who had not yet come to love and know Him, those who had not yet been converted and become new creatures in Christ Jesus.

120

Our Cross

When I was finally able to get one group's attention, they looked at me as one who looks upon a lunatic. "Look. Look," I said, pointing toward the broad and wide road. "Millions upon millions of men and women, young and old, are only a short distance from your cluster. And they are headed right for hell. We have got to do something. Please, please help me to reach them!"

The worship and praise stopped. No one in the group moved. It was like they were in a stupor. Since it seemed like I had their attention, I continued with my exhortation for them to help me reach the lost. Finally, one of the men spoke up. "Excuse me, brother, but God has not given us a spirit of condemnation. It seems to us that you are trying to bring us into bondage with this legalism. Whom the Son has set free is free indeed. You're putting this heavy guilt trip on us, and that definitely cannot be God. And to be quite blunt with you evangelism is not our ministry." For a moment I was totally dumbfounded. Surely this brother in Christ had to be joking. There is no way that anybody could be that ignorant of God's Word and God's heart. For a minute I was in such shock that I could not answer them. The Holy Spirit rose up within me, and out of my mouth came Scripture after Scripture.

> *"And Jesus said unto them, Come ye after me, and I will make you to become fishers of men"* (Mark 1:17).

> *"For the Son of man is come to seek and to save that which was lost"* (Luke 19:10).

I kept pleading and imploring them to help me pull humanity from the flames of hell. But no matter what I said, they did not seem to understand what I was saying. And I could not get them to move. I remember standing there completely frustrated, weeping, and crying uncontrollably. Not only for the damned but for those who called themselves believers.

Somehow the enemy of our souls has deceived the majority of the church into a place of spiritual complacency and pacifism. Now, there is no denying that there is some small measure of concern for the lost. But there's not the red-hot fervency and overwhelming love for souls that we should have. It is so sad that it seems that those within the body of Christ do not believe in hell themselves. God's number one concern is for souls to be saved.

> *"And he said to them all, If any man will come after me, let him deny himself, and take up his cross daily, and follow me" (Luke 9:23).*

Soul winning is the cross that every believer is called of God to carry. God is calling every one of us to win souls. This is what the Scripture means when it says to love your neighbor as you love yourself.

> *"I have planted, Apollos watered; but God gave the increase. So then neither is he that planteth any thing, neither he that watereth; but God that giveth the increase. Now he that planteth and he that watereth are one: and every man shall receive his own reward according to his own labour. For we are labourers together with God: ye are God's husbandry, ye are God's building" (1 Cor. 3:6-9).*

122

Chapter 11
In the Harvest

I fell to my knees on the ground under tremendous sorrow and the heavy burden that was upon my heart, surrounded by these brothers and sisters in Christ. I closed my eyes as I wept with heavy sobs praying that God would open the eyes of humanity and of His church. I prayed that God would forgive me for my lack of concern and love. I prayed that the Lord of the harvest would raise up laborers for the harvest field. How long I prayed, I do not know. When I finally opened up my eyes, I found myself back in my barracks upon my knees in prayer.

Willie Wine was on his knees right off to the side of me. I saw a strange expression on his face. Neither one of us said anything for a while. I noticed there was no music or sound of the men in the background. I asked him what was going on? He told me that they heard me screaming, crying, and wailing in the most unbelievable, heartrending and horrifying ways. He said they were all scared and ran for it. Willie asked me what had happened? During all the hours that I was experiencing this supernatural visitation from the Lord, Willie had been in prayer right at my side. I tried to describe to him everything that happened. Partly due to this visitation, a miniature revival hit our military base.

From that moment forth an overwhelming burden came upon me. My love for Christ and souls went way beyond what I had experienced before. I became extremely desperate to reach souls for Christ. On the streets and highways, malls and shopping centers, Laundromats, and bar rooms. Wherever I could reach people, I was there.

Why This Book?

First, let me say that I never intended to write about this encounter with God. To me, it was extremely personal and overwhelming. When I approached a well-known publishing company to publish a book for me, it was actually for another book. But as I began to share some of my testimony with the lady who is in charge of the acquisitions, she strongly suggested that I should write a book about this experience. Truthfully, I was very reluctant at the beginning. But as she continued to encourage me, I began to see that this was a part of God's plan possibly to stir the hearts of God's people to begin to evangelize in a greater way. Off the top of my head I can quickly count seven benefits to sharing with you my experiences:

1. To create a deeper love and passion for souls!
2. To wake up a sleeping church!
3. For the salvation of sinners.
4. To instigate divine visitations in the lives of fellow believers.
5. That the fear of the Lord might come back into the earth and in into His church.
6. So we might be ready for the final outpouring of the early and latter rain.
7. That revival would break forth in the salvation of souls throughout the body of Christ.

What Will *You* Do?

Brothers and sisters, now that you have been confronted with the reality of masses of people headed to hell, what are *you* going to do about it? Will we become coworkers together with Christ?

> *"But let every man prove his own work, and then shall he have rejoicing in himself alone, and not in another. For every man shall bear his own burden" (Gal. 6:4-5).*

How can we allow humanity, our moms and dads, brothers and sisters, aunts and uncles, sons and daughters, neighbors and friends go to hell without warning them? Without telling them the truth? May God stir up our hearts that we may go forth and proclaim the glorious Good News that Jesus Christ took our place so that we would not have to suffer the penalty of eternal damnation.

It is the will of God for every one of us within the body of Christ to have a burden for souls and to evangelize. It is our responsibility to share the Good News of Jesus Christ.

Note to Sinners and Backsliders

For those who possibly are not right with God, the story I have just shared with you truly happened to me. The Bible says that:

> *"By faith Noah, being warned of God of things not seen as yet, moved with fear, prepared an ark to the saving of his house; by the which he condemned the world, and became heir of the righteousness which is by faith" (Heb. 11:7).*

God is moving in my heart with tremendous love and fear for you and for all of those who might not love God. I beg you and plead with you, in the name of Jesus Christ of Nazareth, to turn from your selfish, sinful, wicked ways and claim a new life in Jesus Christ. Or you will go to a burning hell. Once you have crossed the dark river of death, never more will you see a flower or green pastures or rolling oceans. Never will you again enjoy a glass of clear pure water or the simple pleasures of life. You will never again enjoy the sweet communion with those you love and know. But you will be lost forever in the endless ages of eternal darkness and fire.

Darkness and pain, torment and sorrow will be your eternal destiny. Shaking hands with a preacher will not save you. Putting your name on a church membership list will not do it. Giving money to a ministry or doing good deeds of any kind will not get you to heaven. We must repent of willful, known sin, and we must have a Godly sorrow for our actions. We must ask God, out of the depths of our hearts, to forgive us. And no matter how great our sin is, if we are sincere and no longer want to stay in our sins, God will deliver and forgive and accept us. Oh, sinner, be warned while there is yet time, and the eyes of the Savior still plead, and Jesus still beckons. Leave the broad and wide path of a selfish life, which leads to hell. And walk upon the straight and narrow way, which leads to heaven.

Remember how the demons cried out and asked Jesus whether He had come to torment them before their time? Are we so foolish as to not be moved by the realities of hell or to make light of them? Christianity consists of a new heart and a new life, dedicated and committed to not sinning. It is living for the glory of God. If your heart and life has not been changed by God, if you are still living in open rebellion and known disobedience to the Word and will of God, and you are not concerned about it, you have no right to assume you are going to heaven. The devil and his demons will have the right to grab you by the hair, by your arms and legs, and pull you to hell with them. Sin is worse than hell because sin made it necessary for Jesus to

126

create such a place called hell. It is the ultimate conclusion of a sinful life. Please, flee from sin! Flee from living for your self. Flee from being self-pleasing, self-serving, self-loving, and self-centered. When you die, it will be too late too turn away from your sins. All opportunity to turn to God ends at death. Unless you turn from your selfishness and run to Jesus Christ and believe on Him who is our only hope, you will curse God eternally. And you will never die to the pains, agonies, terrors, horrors, and sorrows of hell. You will never experience the glory of heaven.

> *"Many will say to me in that day, Lord, Lord, have we not prophesied in thy name? and in thy name have cast out devils? and in thy name done many wonderful works? and then will I profess unto them, I never knew you: depart from me, ye that work iniquity"* (Matt. 7:22).

I pray with all of my heart that this experience God allowed me to have in order to warn you will cause you to look to the loving Savior who poured out His lifeblood for you and who was nailed to the cross for your sins. He lovingly and longingly desires you to become one of His children. Won't you believe upon Him today? Call out to Him today. He will in no way cast out any who come to Him. Please, please turn from your wicked, evil, and self-centered ways. Love Him who first loved us. Let God give you a new heart and nature, a heart that loves, serves, and follows God. I hope to see you in heaven!

Chapter 12
My Journey to Heaven

The description of my journey to heaven will be much briefer than that which I experienced when I went to hell. The reason for this is that there are many things the Lord spoke to my heart and revealed to me, things that are "not lawful" for me to share.

> "How that he was caught up into paradise, and heard unspeakable words, which it is not lawful for a man to utter" (2 Cor. 12:4).

> "And the vision of the evening and the morning which was told is true: wherefore shut thou up the vision; for it shall be for many days" (Dan. 8:26).

This divine, angelic visitation happened approximately one month after I had gone to hell. This time I was all alone praying and crying out to God in our dormitory. I had been walking around with my hands in the air praying, singing, and talking to the Lord. Suddenly, my room was filled with an overwhelming presence of the Lord. It was so real that I fell to my knees and tears began to flow freely from my eyes. I found myself lying flat upon my face totally caught up in this overwhelming presence. My face was buried into the floor. I was weeping, crying, and praying. All of a sudden the room I was in was filled with an intense bright light. I lifted my head to see what in the world was going on. There in front of me was a portal. It was like an opening into another world. It was not square like a regular door opening. This doorway was circular on the top like an archway. The light coming from this portal was so bright and brilliant that I could not really even look at it.

I was completely petrified and did not know what to do. It felt as if I was frozen to the floor and unable even to move a muscle. A holy fear gripped my whole body. I could see that someone was walking toward me through this tunnel of light. Out of this glorious light stepped a figure of a man. This was no ordinary man. He was about seven feet tall with a broad chest and shoulders but a slender waist. His flesh blazed like the burning of an arch welder, and he had dark hair. His face did not seem to have ever been shaved. In other words, there was no stubble on his face. He had the stature of a body builder only more solid and almost unearthly. He wore a glistening, brilliant, white gown with a slightly transparent belt around his waist that glowed of silver. I was not able to move or talk in his presence. When this angelic being finally spoke to me his voice seemed to fill the whole room. He said to me, "Fear not; for I have come from the presence of the Almighty to show you things that must come to pass."

I remember asking him, "What is your name?" He replied, "My name is of no importance. I am but a messenger sent to you with a message and a mission that is greater than I." Inwardly, I wondered what kind of purpose could there be in this visitation. As I reflect upon this experience, I will tell you that parts of it is missing from my memory. It's not that it was not real or substantial. It is because it is sealed away in my heart.

And I am not able or permitted to reveal or repeat all that transpired.

The angel spoke to me and said, "Now you must come with me. For there are many things you must see." This angel stepped forward, leaned down, and took me by the hand. He lifted me to my feet. The way he lifted me up I must have been as light as a feather in his hands. It was as if he rippled with unlimited strength. I was like a little child in his hand. I knew in my heart that he could easily kill me without any effort. This was my first experience in a tangible way with an angelic being. From that time up to now I have been protected, provided through and helped by these amazing messengers of God. For instance, I'm convinced an angelic being drove my car for many hours once when I was totally caught up praising and worshiping God as I drove down the road with my hands off the steering wheel.

"Bless the LORD, ye his angels, that excel in strength, that do his commandments, hearkening unto the voice of his word" (Ps. 103:20).

I remember holding his hand with my right hand. There was tremendous heat coming from it. It was not the same type of heat I had experienced in hell. It is almost impossible to explain to you the sensations and feelings I was experiencing at that moment. The fire I felt in his hand was a holy fire. It seemed as if the heat was a living thing. Power radiated from his body. I cannot remember the color of his eyes. This angel was not Jesus. He was simply a messenger sent to take me into the heavens.

"Who maketh his angels spirits; his ministers a flaming fire" (Ps. 104:4).

"Are they not all ministering spirits, sent forth to minister for them who shall be heirs of salvation?" (Heb. 1:14).

Portal to Heaven

I found myself being led by this angel into the portal doorway of brilliant light. As I stepped into this light, the light flooded my whole being. All of the filthiness of the flesh felt as if it just melted right off of me. For the first time in my life I felt completely pure and holy. At that moment I was literally transformed—soul, mind, and body! My mind became extremely clear and more comprehensive than I had ever thought possible. A whole new world opened up to me spiritually, mentally, and emotionally. Another thing I noticed was that when I stepped into this portal, time itself seemed to come to a complete standstill; it became eternity. How I knew this, I do not know. It was something I simply knew without any doubt. Virtual truths began to flood my innermost being. As I stood in this light, things that I could not possibly have any way of knowing were imparted into my soul.

As a result of this experience, I believe that my spiritual growth was accelerated beyond all natural reason. The proof of this is that the last thirty years God has allowed me to go places and do things I could not have done in my own ability. This is not the first time in history something like this has transpired. Solomon is a good example. God supernaturally imparted into Solomon understanding and wisdom that he would never have attained through natural means. (We might call this a "download" into Solomon.) Read the book of proverbs.

"And God gave Solomon wisdom and understanding exceeding much, and largeness

of heart, even as the sand that is on the sea shore. And Solomon's wisdom excelled the wisdom of all the children of the east country, and all the wisdom of Egypt. For he was wiser than all men; than Ethan the Ezrahite, and Heman, and Chalcol, and Darda, the sons of Mahol: and his fame was in all nations round about. And he spake three thousand proverbs: and his songs were a thousand and five. And he spake of trees, from the cedar tree that is in Lebanon even unto the hyssop that springeth out of the wall: he spake also of beasts, and of fowl, and of creeping things, and of fishes. And there came of all people to hear the wisdom of Solomon, from all kings of the earth, which had heard of his wisdom" (1 Kings 4:29-34).

In the late 1800s to the early 1900s there was a woman minister by the name of Marie Woodworth-Etter. It was said that in one moment God gave her mind the ability to remember the whole Bible. On a much smaller scale, I myself have experienced something similar. In 1996 I was convicted to begin to memorize books of the Bible. So I memorized the book of Ephesians. It took many hours and days. After Ephesians I memorized the book of Galatians. This took a lot of natural work because my mind did not want to cooperate. I was never known to be a very brilliant or intelligent person. I quit high school when I was fifteen years old. I was always at the bottom of my class even in the military.

After I gave my heart to Christ, He supernaturally enabled me to do things beyond my natural abilities. But I still was not what you would call exceptional. After the books of Ephesians and Galatians, I memorized the book of Philippians. In the process of doing this I experienced tremendous headaches. But I did not let up. As I was halfway through the book of Colossians, something supernatural happened. I had what the Bible would call an open vision. The room I was standing in disappeared. And in front of me was a large brilliant blue body of water. There was not one ripple or wave upon this water. The sky above me was a bright light blue. There was not one cloud in the sky. As I was looking up into this realm, I saw what looked like a crystal clear raindrop falling from the heavens. It was falling in slow motion. I saw it spinning very slow, changing its shape as it fell. I tracked it with my eyes as it fell from the heavens toward this body of water. When it finally hit the surface of this water, it sent small ripples out, which became larger waves across the water.

At that very moment I could feel my brain expanding. The vision disappeared, but this sensation of my mind expanding continued. As I continued to work on memorizing the book of Colossians, to my utter amazement I discovered that my mind had become like a sponge. It became almost photogenic. Where previously it would take ten to twenty hours or longer to memorize a chapter of the Bible, I could now memorize it in less than an hour. I quickly memorized nine books of the New Testament, not including thousands of other Scriptures.

I'm sorry to say, though, that I became so busy running the church, Christian school, a small bible college, radio station, TV broadcasting and construction projects, twenty-two churches in the Philippines, not including other aspects of being a pastor, that I did not continue in memorizing the Bible. Through the years though, I've had an insatiable hunger for the Word of God. God has allowed me to write over five thousand sermons and to do many things that I never have been taught or trained in. In the midst of all these activities I have earned a PhD in biblical theology and have received a Doctorate of Divinity. I believe it is all because of divine supernatural visitations and the quickening of God's Spirit. The reason why I believe we do not experience more of these visitations is because of a lack of spiritual hunger. If we would hunger and thirst, God would satisfy these desires.

> *"Blessed are they which do hunger and thirst after righteousness: for they shall be filled"* (Matt 5:6).

> *"Delight thyself also in the LORD; and he shall give thee the desires of thine heart. Commit thy way unto the LORD; trust also in him; and he shall bring it to pass. And he shall bring forth thy righteousness as the light, and thy judgment as the noonday"* (Ps. 37:4-6).

Tunnel of Light

The light in this tunnel was just as bright, but it no longer hurt my eyes. Before me laid a seemingly never-ending corridor. The walls, floor, and ceiling of this tunnel were made of tangible light. I was literally walking on or in a beam of light. The walls and floor were actually real. This long corridor of light seemed to be headed upward on a slight incline toward the heavens. The angel and I began to walk up this long corridor together with him holding my hand as if I was a little child. We seemed to walk together like this forever. It felt like a never-ending walk, yet I never got tired or weary. Actually it was extremely pleasant. After what appeared to be a noticeable length of time the angelic being just disappeared. I did not know exactly when he disappeared. One minute he was at my side, and the next minute I realized he was gone. Not knowing what else to do, I kept on walking.

Now even though the angel was no longer with me, I did not feel all alone for I could sense that God was right there at my side, maybe not in the physical form but by His spiritual overwhelming presence. Something else strange was happening. Even though I was walking at a normal pace, it seemed like I was moving extremely fast. It was like I was on a high-speed escalator. It makes me laugh now, but I think I was going at the speed of light. At the same time both my mind and heart were experiencing an overwhelming peace and joy. There were no fears, cares, sin, or sorrow, just total harmony and serenity of spirit, soul, mind, and body. All of my past was gone as if it never existed. All of the struggles and wrestling, fears and anxieties, were gone. It was absolute heavenly bliss. I cannot describe how incredible I felt. In all of my imaginations I never thought someone could feel as good as I was feeling. In hell there is nothing but pain and suffering. But in heaven there is nothing but pleasure and awesome peace.

Chapter 13
Garden of Eden

The next thing I knew, I was out of this tunnel of light. I found myself standing on a tall hill covered with emerald green grass. I had entered into a place so beautiful and incredible that it temporarily took my breath away. There, stretched out before me as far as my eyes could see, was a majestic and indescribable world. Right below me was the most perfect valley you could imagine. What I was looking upon is beyond the comprehension of human description or imagination. There were snow-capped mountains just off to the left of me, rolling hills to the right, and the valley that was below me was amazingly picturesque. In this valley was a beautiful river. In the distance there was an incredible forest filled with trees greater then the redwoods in California.

"But as it is written, Eye hath not seen, nor ear heard, neither have entered into the heart of man, the things which God hath prepared for them that love him. But God hath revealed them unto us by his Spirit: for the Spirit searcheth all things, yea, the deep things of God"
(1 Cor. 2:9-10).

Everywhere I looked there was an abundance of life! There were plants, animals, and insects. God is the Creator and Author of all life. Just by what He has created, you can tell He loves life! In the first two chapters of Genesis we get a glimpse of God's perfect will. I almost laugh every time somebody questions whether or not there could be life on other planets. If the Lord should tarry and we would have an opportunity to thoroughly examine the heavenly bodies, we will discover life even on asteroids. Granted it may be microscopic. But it would still be life. I could even believe that there is life living in the vacuum of space itself.

"And God saw every thing that he had made, and, behold, it was very good. And the evening and the morning were the sixth day" (Gen. 1:31).

The grass upon the hill and much of the valley was a deep emerald green. It was the perfect length, not too low and not too high. Across the valley I could see wheat fields blowing in the wind. Upon the hillsides and plains were beautiful flowers growing in perfect uniformity, as if a gardener with the most exquisite taste had planted each and every one of them. There were amazing, beautiful bushes and hedges as well as plants of every description, size, and shape. Even though through the years I have loved and enjoyed nature, I have never been one to really memorize the names and types of trees, flowers, and plants. The mass majority of the things I saw I could not give you names for, but they were everywhere in abundance.

As I said, in the distance I could see that there was a large forest of trees that were gigantic in proportion. These were redwoods, but they were taller and wider than the redwood forests in Oregon or California, reaching to the heavens above. I have lived in California and Oregon, and there is no denying the beauty of the redwood forests located there. But there is absolutely no comparison between these redwood trees and the ones that are there.

All the plants, animals, and everything I beheld were absolutely perfect in their beauty and completeness. The greatest artist that has ever lived could never imagine what I was now seeing and experiencing.

As I gazed across the landscape, I saw animals large and small, too numerous to count. There were deer, rabbits, and lions eating grass. A small family of bears was splashing in the river, which seemed almost transparent. This river flowed down from a snow-white mountain range unlike any on earth. It was almost like a zoo, but with none of the cages and fences to keep you separated from the animals. It may sound like it was crowded with the description I am sharing with you. But this was not the case. All of the animal and plant life was scattered across the horizon in such an amazing and splendid picturesque way. The river that tumbled its way down the mountainside created waterfalls here and there, until it found its way down to the valley seeking the lowest place of gravity. As the water fell from the side of this mountain, it created a half a dozen or so multicolored rainbows that stood out as if they were three-dimensional.

I have no words to describe the beauty of which I was seeing. I stood frozen in place, overcome with what lay in front of me. I was in a garden that must have been very similar to the Garden of Eden in the book of Genesis. Of course it has not been inhabited by the human race since they were expelled from it. Two cherubim were assigned to stand before its gates. They were to bar the entrance of man from coming back into the garden, in order to prevent him from eating of the tree of life. Wherever I was, it was beautiful!

> *"Therefore the LORD God sent him forth from the garden of Eden, to till the ground from whence he was taken. So he drove out the man; and he placed at the east of the garden of Eden Cherubims, and a flaming sword which turned every way, to keep the way of the tree of life"* (Gen. 3:23-24).

But once you leave Earth as God's people, not only is the Garden of Eden opened to us once more but also the tree of life. I did not see another human being in this place or even signs that there had been people living there. Yet I was not lonely in any aspect of the word. The very air was permeated with such an overwhelming reality of God. The Holy Spirit had to be enabling me to continue to stand upon my feet. Otherwise I surely would have fallen on my face because of the awesomeness of God's presence.

> *"Then I arose, and went forth into the plain: and, behold, the glory of the LORD stood there, as the glory which I saw by the river of Chebar: and I fell on my face"* (Ezek. 3:23).

> *"And when I saw him, I fell at his feet as dead. And he laid his right hand upon me, saying unto me, Fear not; I am the first and the last"* (Rev. 1:17).

Animal Kingdom

Botanists are scientists who study plants. *Zoologists* are those who study animals. *Naturalists* study animals, plants, humans, and nature. *Herpetologists* study reptiles and amphibians. *Ichthyologists* study fish. And *Entomologists* study insects and spiders.

The reason I bring up the names of these specialists is because if they would have been there with me, they would've had the time of their lives. They would have seen all the wonders of Earth's absolute perfection.

Biologists today generally classify all living things into five kingdoms. Two of these are the familiar plant and animal kingdoms. The other three are comprised mainly of very small organisms, like bacteria, larger single-celled creatures, and fungi. The animal kingdom has by far the most species, well over a million. There are over four hundred thousand known plant species, most of which are flowering plants with seeds, such as trees, grasses, and the like. The latter comprise more than a quarter of a million different species. The other three kingdoms contain at least a few hundred thousand different life forms.

The animal kingdom is divided into about thirty phyla. The nine largest phyla contain the majority of species. Indeed, one phyla, the arthropods, which includes insects and spiders, constitutes about 75 percent of all known animal species. More than nine hundred thousand arthropods have been described, and according to some estimates there may be more than five million more.

The number of known species for all animals other than arthropods is about 250,000. The largest group (formally "class") within the phyla of arthropods and the most diverse class in all kingdoms, is insects. Over 750,000 have been described. Some suppose that there are perhaps as many as three million different species of insects in the world.

The most diverse family of insect is beetles, with over 375,000 types identified. Other large families of insects include butterflies and moths (more than one hundred thousand species), bees and wasps (more than twenty thousand species), and ants (about ten thousand species). With over thirty thousand known species, spiders, which are not insects, constitute one of the large families of other kinds of arthropods. Only two other phyla within the animal kingdom, the roundworms and the mollusks, are known to contain more than one hundred thousand species. All other phyla generally have far less.

The dominant phyla on the planet, the vertebrates, consists of less than fifty thousand known species. The number of fish species is estimated to be more than twenty thousand, bird species number approximately 8,700, reptiles about 6,000, mammals about 4,500, and amphibians about 2,500. Within mammals, the rodents are the most varied order, with thirty-four families and more than 1,700 species. [20]

I am sharing this scientific information with you to help expand your horizon that you might better understand who God really is. God is so creative and so full of life that there is no end to His creative ability. These are all natural things that we can discover with the human eye. What myriad of angels, angelic beings, and spiritual beings exist that we cannot see or perceive? Millions? Billions? Trillions? Who can say? From my study of the Scriptures I have discovered at least ten different types of angels. This is by no means meant to be in any way, form, or fashion a complete list.

1. Cherubim: Genesis 3:24; Ezekiel 1:5-28; 28:12, 13, 17; 8:1-4; 10:1-22

2. Seraphim: Isaiah 6:1-7

3. Archangels: Colossians 1:15-18; 1 Thessalonians 4:16; Jude 9

4. Common angels: Matthew 1:20-29; 2:13-19; 28:2-5; Acts 5:19; 8:26; 10:3; 12:7

5. Guardian angels: Psalm 91:12

6. Ministering angels: 1 Kings 19:5-7

7. Avenging angels: Genesis 19:1-29

8. Death angels: Exodus 12:23; Revelation 6:8

9. Living creatures: Revelation 4:6-5:14; 6:1-8; 7:11; 14:3, 9-11; 15:7; 19:4

10. Messengers: similar to the one that came to me

Many people have questions about animals. What happens to animals when they die? Do animals have souls? Almost every question I believe that we have pertaining to life is found within the Scriptures. All we need is to rightly divide the Word of truth by the Holy Spirit. First we understand the animals came from the earth.

"And God said, Let the earth bring forth the living creature after his kind, cattle, and creeping thing, and beast of the earth after his kind: and it was so. And God made the beast of the earth

*after his kind, and cattle after their kind, and
every thing that creepeth upon the earth after
his kind: and God saw that it was good"
(Gen. 1:24-25).*

The following Scripture would imply that the spirit (the
soul) of an animal returns to the earth from whence it came:

*"Who knoweth the spirit of man that goeth
upward, and the spirit of the beast that goeth
downward to the earth?" (Eccles. 3:21).*

All animals belong to God and are made for His pleasure.

*"For every beast of the forest is mine, and the
cattle upon a thousand hills. I know all the
fowls of the mountains: and the wild beasts of
the field are mine" (Ps. 50:10-11).*

Divine Orchestra

In this place called heaven, my hearing had become
extremely sensitive. I had been so overwhelmed by what I
was seeing, it had escaped my attention what I was also
hearing. My ears seemed to be able to pick up sounds
that were miles away. Not only could I hear everything,
but also I could distinguish every sound. I literally could
hear the bees going from one flower to another collecting
pollen. I heard a slight breeze blowing through the grass
on the plains and a cow and its calf chewing their cud.
A lion in the distance roared, not with the ferociousness
of a vicious meat eater but of a lion that was relishing
its existence in harmony with its other fellow creatures.
I could even hear rabbits skipping across the grass. I
heard all of these distinct individual sounds, yet it was

not annoying or confusing like the mad rushing about that goes on in the cities of men. It sounded more like a beautiful orchestra being conducted by a divinely gifted maestro. Such a symphony has never been heard upon Earth since the fall of man.

Supernatural Eyesight

At almost the same time, I noticed the vibrant and vivid colors. They were of such deepness, clarity, and brilliance. Everything was astonishingly three-dimensional. All of the artistic geniuses of this day and age could never even create on paper anything as near to perfection as this was. After this supernatural experience, everything in this world seems to be dim and surreal to me. We may not be able to realize the fullest capacity at this moment, but the spiritual world is more real than the physical world that we live in.

Not only was there incredible supernatural clarity to my sight and hearing but also to my sense of smell, taste, and touch. It all seemed to be magnified a thousandfold. If you could compare these two worlds side-by-side, it would reveal the blandness, the ugliness of the natural world we live in. It is all because of the corruption of sin. The satanic seed that says "my will be done."

But this place of glorious beauty simply revealed the exquisiteness of all that God had created. The aromas that floated in the atmosphere filled my nostrils. The smells were very strong but not at all nauseating; it was quite the opposite. I could even taste to some degree through the sense of my smell. It was one of many delightful experiences that I was encountering in this heavenly place. All of these things registered in my mind, and I knew that I was in heaven. In all of my imaginations of what heaven would be like, never once did it occur to me that it would be like this. Revelation knowledge flowed through my soul as I came to realize God's original plan for man. The earth was to be a miniature version of God's divine habitation. But man's rebellion, his disobedience in yielding his soul to Satan, opened the door to disaster, pestilence, disease, perversion, and corruption. Which turned the earth into a tragic mockery of God's original plan. What was meant to be heaven on earth had become a hellish nightmare.

Chapter 14
Upon a New Road

While pondering these thoughts, I noticed that there was a road that wound its way down through the valley. It was headed in the direction of the gigantic redwood forest. Instinctively my feet began to move me down the hill toward this road. When I finally arrived at it, I looked back from where I came from and realized that I had walked miles and miles. Amazingly, I felt just as relaxed as when I first began, if not even more so. When I reached this road, I discovered that it was built with beautiful multi-colored flat stones, intricately laid together side by side. These stones look like highly polished marble filled with many gold speckles. The road glistened and simmered as if it was wet and slippery. Yet when I stepped upon it I discovered that it was not slippery or wet at all. There were quite a number of different types of animals alongside as well as on the road. None of them fled from me as I walked past them. It was as if all creation was in harmony, and I was not a stranger. Rather, I was an intricate an intimate part of this heavenly place. There was absolutely no fear toward me in these animals that I walked past. Neither was there any fear whatsoever in my heart toward them.

It would've been so wonderful to stop and spend some time petting and playing with these animals. It also would have been nice to walk down through the meadows, to sit by the bank of the beautiful river that was flowing not too far from the road just to let my feet soak in the crystal clear waters. It would have been wonderful to sit down and watch all of the different types of fish that were probably swimming in this crystal-clear river. If only I could just stay right there forever.

Yet there was a deep urgency in my heart. There was something that must transpire while I was there. I knew I was not there just for a foretaste of the future. That God had brought me to this place to show me something pertaining to my purpose in life and humanity was certain. I knew instinctively that what God wanted to show me was somewhere along this road that I was walking upon. I finally reached this majestic forest of redwood trees. The tops of these trees must have been reaching anywhere from two hundred to three hundred feet in the air. There were also smaller trees scattered throughout these giants of the forest. Their circumferences were anywhere from three feet to forty feet in dimension. It was simply mind-boggling.

I stepped into this forest walking upon the multi-colored road. As I came under the towering canopy of these trees, I felt myself being enfolded and wrapped up with comfort and security. How can I describe what I was experiencing at that moment? Without being misunderstood I would like to say that it was magical and mystical. Walt Disney himself would be blown away. None of his children's movies ever came close to what I was experiencing now. Light filtered down through the branches here and there causing shimmering reflections of light to shine off of the leaves of other trees that were growing under the huge canopy. The ground, tree trunks, and large rocks and boulders were covered with many colors of moss. The moss was exquisitely placed as if by professional design. Ferns, some large and many small, stretched through the forest in perfect arrangement. I did not see any thistles or thorns. This place had never experienced the curse of sin.

The path led straight into the heart of the forest. There were no bends or turns as far as my eyes could see. It was as straight as an arrow flies. I walked down this path at an easy rate taking in as much as I could. It was as if I was walking on a cloud. It seemed to be dreamlike and yet it was tangible and touchable. Once in a while, there would be a stone bridge on the path. The stone bridges were made of the same stones as the road itself. The bridges took me over bubbling, sparkling, and transparent water. At one of these streams I stopped for a moment and looked over the bridge into the water. As I looked into the water I could see schools of fish swimming by. They were bright and beautiful like coral reef fish back on Earth, but they were much more exquisite and stunning. The water was so clear that it looked like the fish were swimming in the air. As I continued to walk, my heart overflowed with love for the One who created all of this. As I recall this account, I still get spiritual chills flowing through me.

How far and how long I walked I could not guess. I do know that it was long enough to expect that the sun would be going down. However, there was no change in the light. It was just as bright as when I had first arrived. As I reflected upon this wonder, it dawned upon me that I had not seen the sun in the sky. That the light seemed to be coming from nowhere and yet everywhere! This light did not hurt my eyes. Actually, it was as if my eyes were drinking deep of the light. It was extremely strange and delightful. My eyes were absorbing and pulling in this wonderful light.

The Birds of Heaven

As I continued to walk, everything was so amazingly peaceful and tranquil. Majestic trees stood to the left and right of the approximately twenty-foot wide path. I found myself praising and worshiping God. I discovered that God

149

also had transformed my voice. I could hardly believe how good I could sing. And with this new voice I began to sing with all of my heart my love for the One who meant everything. I was so at home, at peace, and in harmony with this place that I never wanted to leave. I belonged here. I knew I was made to live here forever, that this was my natural environment. As I continued to walk, sing, and worship, the trees began to be filled with birds, thousands upon thousands of birds. The light filtering in between the trees glistened on these birds which were of such magnificent beauty and variety. There were large and small birds of colors and species beyond count. Cockatoos, canaries, doves, parakeets, and finches came just to name a few. Their voices echoed throughout the forest. I knew in my heart that they were singing praises to God. It made you want to be able to join in with them. As I kept on walking, I was completely and totally surrounded by them. It was so overwhelming that I could not walk any further. I just stood there caught up in the majesty and the beauty of it all. They were all lifting their voices in praise, worship, adoration, and love for the Author of life.

Divine Commission

I was so caught up in the wonder and beauty of it all that I did not even notice the angel who had been with me at the start of this journey had returned. He was standing alongside me, gazing at the birds in the trees. The angel asked, "Do you see all of these splendid and beautiful birds?" Surprisingly, I was not at all startled or surprised by the return of this angel. In heaven there is no fear, sickness, or sin. There is nothing but joy, peace, and tranquility beyond description. I turned and spoke to the angel not as a superior but as a fellow companion in the plan and purposes of God. "Sir," I said, "Do you not think that these birds are the most beautiful and amazing creatures you have ever heard or seen?" The angel asked, "Do you understand what it is the Lord God is revealing to you?" When the angel said this to me, I turned once again and looked up directly into his face. I said to him, "What do you mean?" And then this angel said something to me that still overwhelms me to this day. As I share this part of my experience with you, I am almost to the point of weeping. Deep, deep feelings are stirring and moving in my heart. For God was about to reveal His divine commission for my life, the purpose for which Jesus rescued me.

"These birds you are looking upon and listening to are a type, and a shadow of those things which will come to be in and through your life. Even as these birds are of so many different species and colors, so in your future will you have an impact upon many cultures and tongues and nations."

At this statement my mind seemed to go numb for a moment. It just did not seem to make sense. I remember saying, "I don't understand what you mean." He replied, "Servant of the Most High, be it known to you that what you see is a shadow of the souls of men and women who will be brought into the kingdom because of your obedience and hunger for the Lord. Many will be set free from the bondage of sin. Multitudes of many nations, tongues, and tribes will hear the glorious truth, and this truth will set them free. They in turn will go forth in the power and presence of the Holy Spirit and will take the name of Jesus, even as you have done and will do. They will drive back the forces of the adversary. For the day of the Lord is at hand, and a new day is about to dawn. Strengthen your heart. Be strong in the Lord and the power of His might. Hold up the arms of your brethren; wash their feet. Humble yourself. Be a servant, and the Lord will use you. Help those who are called and chosen but have none to assist them. Undergird and encourage them to fulfill the call of God upon their lives."

The words of this messenger of God penetrated my heart to its deepest core. I fell to my knees, then to my face, crying and weeping uncontrollably. God had spoken to me. I would never be the same again! The Lord did have a divine purpose for my life. I was called of God and sent forth by the Almighty to set others free. Instantly, in my heart I knew that it was not about me. I knew that I was only one small gear in the majestic machinery of God's divine plan. My heart was filled with joy unspeakable and full of glory. How long I lay there on that road and cried and wept, I do not know. The next thing I realized was that the angel was gone, and I was no longer in the woods.

Chapter 15
Before the Throne

Next I found myself in an immense never-ending realm. So large was this place that I could not see an ending. Above me, behind me, to the left and the right just seemed to be a never-ending horizon. The floor under my feet was like a sea of crystal glass radiating and pulsating with ever-changing colors that flowed through it like an incoming wave of the ocean. In the distance, I saw lightning and extremely bright flashes of light proceeding from one point. Not knowing what else to do, I began to move toward this phenomenon. As I drew closer, I heard thunder echoing off in the distance which sounded like mighty trumpets. The sea of glass under my feet shook with every peel of lightning. And with every step I took toward this phenomenon, my heart beat faster. It was as if the hair on the back of my neck and up my arms and head were standing straight up.

In the far distance I could see that I was approaching what looked like a huge throne. In front of the throne and around it, there seemed to be some type of activity that was transpiring. As I got closer I began to discern the most awesome creatures I could have ever imagine. Yet my attention was not on them. The Scriptures declare that there are four of them altogether, full of eyes before and behind. The first is like a lion, the second like a calf, the third has the face of a man, and the fourth beast is like a flying eagle. They each have six wings and on the inside of the wings they are full of eyes. When I was still a great way off, even before I saw them, I heard these beasts declaring with a loud voice, "Holy, holy, holy, Lord God Almighty, Who was and Who is and Who is to come." (Up to this point many of these things I am relating to you seemed to have vanished from my mind. But even as I am retelling it all, once again it grips my heart.)

My eyes were on the One on the throne. I could tell that the throne was amazing. But even more majestic and splendid than the throne was the One who sat upon it. He appeared like the brightness of translucent diamonds. A light shined out of the One on the throne that was of such an intensity and holiness. Had I not been in the spirit, it would have killed me, consumed me, burned me up, and evaporated me into nothingness. At the right side sat Jesus, clothed with a robe down to His feet, and about His chest He had a breastplate of glistening gold like that of a Roman general. His hair radiated like glistening white wool, more pure than the whitest snow. His eyes burned with divine love as if flames of fire. Streaks of lightning were flashing all around the throne. The roar of thunder continued.

> *"And in the midst of the seven candlesticks one like unto the Son of man, clothed with a garment down to the foot, and girt about the paps with a golden girdle. His head and his hairs were white like wool, as white as snow; and his eyes were as a flame of fire; And his feet like unto fine brass, as if they burned in a furnace; and his voice as the sound of many waters. And he had in his right hand seven stars: and out of his mouth went a sharp twoedged sword: and his countenance was as the sun shineth in his strength" (Rev. 1:13-16).*

I knew without a shadow of doubt that I stood before God the Father and His Son, Jesus Christ. Around about them and stretching over the top of them shone numerous emerald rainbows much clearer and colorful than the natural mind could conceive.

"After this I looked, and, behold, a door was opened in heaven: and the first voice which I heard was as it were of a trumpet talking with me; which said, Come up hither, and I will shew thee things which must be hereafter. And immediately I was in the spirit: and, behold, a throne was set in heaven, and one sat on the throne. And he that sat was to look upon like a jasper and a sardine stone: and there was a rainbow round about the throne, in sight like unto an emerald. And round about the throne were four and twenty seats: and upon the seats I saw four and twenty elders sitting, clothed in white raiment; and they had on their heads crowns of gold. And out of the throne proceeded lightnings and thunderings and voices: and there were seven lamps of fire burning before the throne, which are the seven Spirits of God. And before the throne there was a sea of glass like unto crystal: and in the midst of the throne, and round about the throne, were four beasts full of eyes before and behind. And the first beast was like a lion, and the second beast like a calf, and the third beast had a face as a man, and the fourth beast was like a flying eagle. And the four beasts had each of them six wings about him; and they were full of eyes within: and they rest not day and night, saying, Holy, holy, holy, Lord God Almighty, which was, and

is, and is to come. And when those beasts give glory and honour and thanks to him that sat on the throne, who liveth for ever and ever, The four and twenty elders fall down before him that sat on the throne, and worship him that liveth for ever and ever, and cast their crowns before the throne, saying, Thou art worthy, O Lord, to receive glory and honour and power: for thou hast created all things, and for thy pleasure they are and were created" (Rev. 4:1-11).

I fell as one dead before the throne, quivering and shaking before the presence of my Lord. Then a voice spoke forth as if coming from everywhere. It filled my mind and heart with shaking and trembling. This voice was filled with absolute complete and total authority and holiness. I knew it was the Father's voice that was speaking to me. As I lay on my face before the throne of God, I heard unspeakable words that could not be uttered with human vocabulary. It was literally as if streaks of lightning were hitting my body with every word that He spoke. As His words hit my body they would explode in me like the soundings of thunder. My whole body literally shook and vibrated uncontrollably at these thunderings. These thunderings flooded my body and took a hold of me. It had to be God supernaturally strengthening me in order to keep me alive through this experience.

I am convinced that if you had been standing at a distance you would have seen streaks of divine lightning and fire striking my body. This divine lightning and fire was not meant to destroy me but to some extent was meant to impregnate me with God's divine purposes and abilities.

I knew that my inner man was drinking deep of the mysteries and divine plans of God. I remember the tears flowing from my eyes, down my face as I listened to the

Word of the Lord. The glory of God was all around, upon, and in me. My body was enveloped in a glistening cloud of energy. Through this whole experience I laid there whispering "Thank you, Jesus," over and over. I did not truly understand with my mind what was transpiring, but I knew in my heart that God was speaking to me divine truths and mysteries, that which was to be accomplished and would shortly come to pass. I knew that He was supernaturally imparting into me the grace that was necessary to accomplish His purposes for my life. This seemed to go on forever. And then as quickly as it had started it was over. The Spirit of the Lord whisked me instantly away from the throne room of God.

Preaching the Gospel

The next place I found myself was on a sidewalk in what looked to be an alleyway of a low-income area of a large city. Coming down the street toward me were two large, rough-looking men. As they caught up to me, I found myself sharing the love and the Good News of Jesus Christ. I also shared the reality of divine judgment if they rejected the sacrificial work of Jesus. As I continued to speak about the reality of Christ and that there is no other way to the Father but through Jesus, I noticed their faces begin to distort until they were filled with absolute, utter hate. Their eyes glistened with a hideous satanic appearance as if they were turning into demons right before my eyes. Before I could even raise my hands in self-defense, they began to hit me in the face and the chest with their fists. After numerous blows, I finally fell to my knees. As I did, they kicked and stomped down on me. In the midst of this persecution, no hatred or malice emanated from my heart for these men that were trying to kill me. My heart and my mind seemed to be completely floating in a sea of love and peace. I found myself crying out loud for them. "Father, please forgive them, for they do not know what they are doing." And then everything went completely black.

When I came to, I found myself lying on the floor of my barracks. I looked around the room expecting to see the angel, but there was no one there but me. It was late in the afternoon. I think approximately at least five hours had come and gone since the angel had first appeared. My experience was not a dream. The reality of everything that had transpired is still eternally embodied in my mind and my heart. I can see it all as clearly as if it had just happened. Whether or not I was in my body or out of it, I cannot tell. I can say this though: without a shadow of a doubt, God has placed a divine mission in my life to perform, a job to do, a purpose to fulfill. By God's grace, nothing will rob me of the reality of it. With all my might, I am determined to fulfill God's will for my life. By God's grace I am not going to disappoint the One who has chosen me to be a soldier in His last day army. I hope you understand that you also have a divine mission and purpose in this life. I pray to God that you will be faithful to that divine call.

> *"And from the days of John the Baptist until now the kingdom of heaven suffereth violence, and the violent take it by force" (Matt. 11:12).*

Chapter 16
The Dream

I had an amazing dream recently. It's very hard to describe in human vernacular. I was sleeping peacefully when, at about three o'clock in the morning, I was suddenly smack dab in the middle of heaven, close to the throne of God. It was so real and tangible; it literally felt as if I was in heaven physically. God gave me eyes to see all of existence. It was as if I was omnipresent. All of creation lay before me. My mind and emotions, and all five of my senses perceived all things. I embraced everything at one time.

It was the most amazing experience you could imagine. It was so beautiful and magnificent that it is beyond precise description. It could be likened to being in the eye of a storm with everything spinning around you. With this supernatural, imparted ability I could perceive the spiritual and angelic. I saw angels of all types and ranks. I saw and felt the nature and the physical realms. I saw the planets, moons, stars, solar systems, and the whole universe. I saw animal life, plant life, oceans, seas, lakes, and rivers. I even saw the microscopic molecular realm. God supernaturally expanded my capacity mentally and emotionally to perceive all things. If it had not happened to me personally, I would be skeptical myself of someone saying these things.

In the midst of this experience I began to be overtaken by an absolute sense of incredible harmony. It

159

was a unity and oneness of a mind-boggling proportion. It resonated through my whole being. I could feel it in my bones, flesh, emotions, and mind. My heart resonated with His harmony. My whole being was engulfed in this unbelievable symphony. All creation, the universe, and spiritual realm was in complete and total harmony and unity. Instantly I perceived everything was at one with God. Not one molecule, not one atom or proton was out of sync with God. As I was looking at creation, suddenly I perceived an invisible force permeating and saturating all of it. God literally gave me eyes to see this invisible force. I could see it moving, flowing, and penetrating everything. With this ability to see, He also gave me spiritual understanding. I realized at that moment that it was this incredible invisible force which was causing all things to exist and flow and move as one living, breathing creation.

What I am sharing with you was a progressive revelation unfolding before me like a flower blossoming. In the midst of this experience my ears opened, and I heard the most incredible music, a breathtaking song. This invisible force was literally a song that was being sung. Instantly I perceived that it was this music, this song, which was holding all of creation together. This song was permeating every animate and inanimate thing together. Not only was it holding everything together but also everything was singing along with it. It was the most incredible music and song you could ever imagine. Actually it is beyond comprehension or human ability to describe this song and what it was doing. All of creation was being upheld and kept together by this song. I could see it and feel it. It was inside of me. I was a part of it. No maestro, psalmist, no Beethoven or Mozart could ever produce such a majestic masterpiece.

As I watched and listened, I was overwhelmed with the reality that it was this song that was causing everything to be in harmony and unity. It was this song causing

160

everything to live, move, exist, and have being. During this experience a curiosity took a hold of me. I began to wonder, where is this music, this song, coming from? I began to look high and low, trying to discover where this song had originated. I finally looked behind me, and on a higher elevation I saw God sitting upon His throne. I did not see the clarity of God's form or face. He was covered in a glistening mist, somewhat like fog. But as I looked upon His form, it was as if my eyes zoomed in on His mouth. I was looking intently at the mouth of God. Out of His mouth was coming this amazing, beautiful, awesome song.

This song that God was singing was holding everything together and in perfect harmony. God the Father was making everything one with Himself through this song, this music coming out of His mouth. I literally could see, feel, and experience the song coming out of God's mouth. In my heart I said to the Father, "Father, how long will You sing this song?" And He spoke to me in my heart, "Throughout eternity, My voice will never cease to sing. My voice will never cease to be heard." I could see letters streaming from God's mouth. Words were coming forth from His mouth. They were swimming in a river of transparent life, like fish swimming in a river. These words seemed to be alive. They were spreading throughout the entire universe, causing everything to exist and to be in harmony. They were permeating all of creation, visible and invisible, spiritual and natural.

I knew in my heart that this was the Word of God, the divinely inspired Scriptures. The Word was swimming as if in an invisible transparent river. I knew that this river was a living, quickening force. I knew that it was this river which was causing the Word of God to be alive. The Word of God was being carried forth by this river. I said to the Father, "Father, what is this river that the Word is flowing, swimming, and living in?" And He said to my heart, "It is the Holy Ghost!"

I was stunned into silence. After a while I repeated my question. Once again He said to me, "It is the Holy Ghost. It is the breath of My mouth coming from the voice of My lips. And this voice is My Son, Jesus Christ. My voice is My Son, Jesus Christ. And out of His voice comes the Holy Ghost and My Word." Further He said to me, "My Word would not sustain, heal, deliver, or bring life unless it is quickened and made alive by My Spirit." Then the Father confirmed this to me by quoting the Scripture where Jesus said, "My Words are Spirit, and they are life." (See John 6:63.) The Father spoke to me again and said, "You can quote, memorize, and declare the whole Bible, but it will be dead and lifeless until you yield, surrender, move, flow, and come into complete harmony with the Word of God and the Holy Ghost."

This I believe, to some extent, reveals God's eternal purpose for you and I: to be in complete oneness and harmony with God, the Father, the Son, and the Holy Ghost!

Chapter 17
Conclusion

I have shared with you from my heart some of the experiences that the Lord has allowed me to go through. I know that what I have shared could never capture to the fullest extent what took place in my journey to hell or my time spent in heaven. But I pray that the Lord has used it to touch your life in some degree. The harvest is truly great, but the laborers are few. I hope this book would become a catalyst that God could use to bring about a supernatural, enabling encounter with Him. If there was ever a time the body of Christ needs to be active, it is now.

"No man that warreth entangleth himself with the affairs of this life; that he may please him who hath chosen him to be a soldier" (2 Tim. 2:4).

You see, God is not a respecter of persons. But every one of us has a different job, a different position, a unique place within the body. Do not believe or accept the lie that God does not have a specific purpose for your life. After God created the heavens and the earth, He put into place a new law. God made it so that man became the gateway, channel, and avenue by which He would move, rule, and reign. There are an overwhelming amount of Scriptures that clearly proclaimed this amazing truth. Hebrews chapter eleven reveals the names of twenty-two people God used to bring about His ultimate purpose and plan. The entire Bible is a declaration that it is now through man that God steps into the midst of humanity. God is looking and searching for men and women who will agree with His heart.

"And God blessed them, and God said unto them, Be fruitful, and multiply, and replenish the earth, and subdue it: and have dominion over the fish of the sea, and over the fowl of the air, and over every living thing that moveth upon the earth" (Gen. 1:28).

"For the prophecy came not in old time by the will of man: but holy men of God spake as they were moved by the Holy Ghost" (2 Pet. 1:21).

The heavenly Father stepped into this world through Jesus Christ to deliver, heal, save, and set men free. He was the physical embodiment of all that the heavenly Father is. He is the answer and solution to all of the world's problems.

"Neither is there salvation in any other: for there is none other name under heaven given among men, whereby we must be saved" (Acts 4:12).

Now it is our turn to be surrendered and submitted to the heavenly Father, His precious Son, and the Holy Ghost. We were made to be possessed, inhabited, filled, and under the influence of the Three in One. God has given to us the opportunity to be coworkers in the harvest field. Let us go forth in His mighty name. By His divine grace, power, authority, and His name may we go forth to set the multitudes free!

Endnotes:

1. (pg. 29)Wikipedia; the Free Encyclopedia, "Parachuting." http://en.wikipedia.org/wiki/Parachuting
2. (pg. 32) USGS/HVO Volcano Watch, November 14, 1997.
3. (pg. 49) The 10 Deadliest Diseases, Elistmania. Posted FairDinkum, byhttp://www.elistmania.com/juice/the_10_deadliest_diseases.
4. (pg. 68) Solomon Benjamin Shaw, *The Dying Testimonies of Saved and Unsaved*, (1898) http://www.biblebelievers.com/dying_testimonies/index.html.
5. (pg. 69) Ibid, 27-28.
6. (pg. 69) Ibid, 65-66.
7. (pg. 69) Ibid, 83.
8. (pg. 70) Ibid, 101.
9. (pg. 70) Ibid, 166.
10. (pg. 71) Ibid, 202.
11. (pg. 71) Ibid, 261.
12. (pg. 71) Ibid, 271.
13 (pg. 72) Near death Experiences and the Afterlife, Reverend Kenneth Hagin. http://www.near-death.com/forum/nde/000/90.html.
14. (pg. 81) The Physics Factbook edited by Glenn Elert, "Number of Nurons in a Human Brain" http://hypertextbook.com/facts/2002/AniciaNdabahaliye2.shtml.
15. (pg. 95) U.S. Census Bureau, World POPClock Projection. www.census.gov/ipc/www/popclockworld.html.
16. (pg. 95) Web Droppings, Little Known Facts 4. http://www.slightlywarped.com/crapfactory/webdroppings/2010/littleknownfacts4.htm.
17. (pg. 95) Near Death Experiences and the Afterlife, Rev. Howard Pittman. http://www.near-death.com/forum/nde/000/89.html.
18. (pg. 104) Wikipedia, the Free Encyclopedia. "Roman Legion." http://en.wikipedia.org/wiki/Roman_legion.
19. (pgs. 111-118) William Booth, A Vision of the Lost, http://www.globalchristians.org/downloads/Church%20History%20Documents/William%20Booth%20vision1.htm.
20. (pg 141-142) The Number of Different Species, http://pages.prodigy.net/jhonig/bignum/qspecies.html.

About the Author

Dr. Michael H. Yeager is a motivated speaker who would love to come and minister to your church or group. You can reach him through the following:

Address:
Jesus is Lord ministries international
3425 Chambersburg Rd.
Biglerville, Pennsylvania 17307

Phone: 1-800-555-4575

Websites:
www.docyeager.org
www.wordbroadcast.org
www.hellsreal.com

Made in the USA
Middletown, DE
28 December 2018